Current
CONTROVERSIES

Carbon Offsets

Other Books in the Current Controversies Series

Carbon Offsets

Debra A. Miller, Book Editor

GREENHAVEN PRESS
A part of Gale, Cengage Learning

Detroit • New York • San Francisco • New Haven, Conn • Waterville, Maine • London

Christine Nasso, *Publisher*
Elizabeth Des Chenes, *Managing Editor*

© 2009 Greenhaven Press, a part of Gale, Cengage Learning

For more information, contact:
Greenhaven Press
27500 Drake Rd.
Farmington Hills, MI 48331-3535
Or you can visit our Internet site at gale.cengage.com

For product information and technology assistance, contact us at

Gale Customer Support, 1-800-877-4253
For permission to use material from this text or product, submit all requests online at www.cengage.com/permissions

Further permissions questions can be emailed to permissionrequest@cengage.com

Articles in Greenhaven Press anthologies are often edited for length to meet page requirements. In addition, original titles of these works are changed to clearly present the main thesis and to explicitly indicate the author's opinion. Every effort is made to ensure that Greenhaven Press accurately reflects the original intent of the authors. Every effort has been made to trace the owners of copyrighted material.

Cover image Frederic J. Brown/AFP/Getty Images.

LIBRARY OF CONGRESS CATALOGING-IN-PUBLICATION DATA

Carbon offsets / Debra A. Miller, book editor.
    p. cm. -- (Current controversies)
    Includes bibliographical references and index.
    ISBN 978-0-7377-4454-5 (hardcover)
    ISBN 978-0-7377-4455-2 (pbk.)
    1. Deforestation--Control--popular works. 2. Afforestation--Environmental aspects--Popular works. 3. Carbon offsetting--Popular works. 4. Carbon offsetting--United States--Popular works. I. Miller, Debra A.
    SD418.C37 2009
    363.738'74--dc22

                                                2008055849

Printed in the United States of America
2 3 4 5 6   26 25 24 23 22

Contents

Chapter 1: How Do Carbon Offsets Work?

Chapter 2: Are Carbon Offsets Effective in Reducing Global Warming?

Chapter 3: Are Tree-Based Carbon Offsets Beneficial?

Chapter Overview
Toni Johnson

Loss of forests contributes significantly to global greenhouse gas emissions, so reducing deforestation has become a priority in international discussions on climate change. Many environmentalists, however, have concerns about including forest projects in carbon offset programs.

Yes, Tree-Based Carbon Offsets Are Beneficial

Carbon Credits Can Encourage Developing
Nations to Protect Trees
Rachel Oliver

Experts have warned that if the world wants to cut carbon emissions, it must stop cutting down so many trees. Carbon offset programs that compensate developing nations for preserving their forests may be one way to accomplish this goal.

Carbon Credits Could Save the Rainforests
Rhett A. Butler

Deforestation reportedly contributes 20–25 percent of greenhouse gas emissions. Initiatives to award carbon credits to developing nations for helping less developed countries protect existing rainforests, which have a great ability to store carbon, could be a win-win situation.

Carbon Offsets for Preventing Deforestation
Could Raise the Value of Living Forests
Science Daily

Researchers in 2007 found that the ventures that prompted deforestation in various areas around the globe frequently generated less than five dollars per ton of carbon released, suggesting that if the emerging market for carbon credits could reward farmers for not cutting down trees, they could prevent a large amount of deforestation.

Chapter 4: How Should the Voluntary Carbon Offset Market Be Regulated?

Foreword

By definition, controversies are "discussions of questions in which opposing opinions clash" (Webster's Twentieth Century Dictionary Unabridged). Few would deny that controversies are a pervasive part of the human condition and exist on virtually every level of human enterprise. Controversies transpire between individuals and among groups, within nations and between nations. Controversies supply the grist necessary for progress by providing challenges and challengers to the status quo. They also create atmospheres where strife and warfare can flourish. A world without controversies would be a peaceful world; but it also would be, by and large, static and prosaic.

The Series' Purpose

The purpose of the Current Controversies series is to explore many of the social, political, and economic controversies dominating the national and international scenes today. Titles selected for inclusion in the series are highly focused and specific. For example, from the larger category of criminal justice, Current Controversies deals with specific topics such as police brutality, gun control, white collar crime, and others. The debates in Current Controversies also are presented in a useful, timeless fashion. Articles and book excerpts included in each title are selected if they contribute valuable, long-range ideas to the overall debate. And wherever possible, current information is enhanced with historical documents and other relevant materials. Thus, while individual titles are current in focus, every effort is made to ensure that they will not become quickly outdated. Books in the Current Controversies series will remain important resources for librarians, teachers, and students for many years.

In addition to keeping the titles focused and specific, great care is taken in the editorial format of each book in the series. Book introductions and chapter prefaces are offered to provide background material for readers. Chapters are organized around several key questions that are answered with diverse opinions representing all points on the political spectrum. Materials in each chapter include opinions in which authors clearly disagree as well as alternative opinions in which authors may agree on a broader issue but disagree on the possible solutions. In this way, the content of each volume in Current Controversies mirrors the mosaic of opinions encountered in society. Readers will quickly realize that there are many viable answers to these complex issues. By questioning each author's conclusions, students and casual readers can begin to develop the critical thinking skills so important to evaluating opinionated material.

Current Controversies is also ideal for controlled research. Each anthology in the series is composed of primary sources taken from a wide gamut of informational categories including periodicals, newspapers, books, U.S. and foreign government documents, and the publications of private and public organizations. Readers will find factual support for reports, debates, and research papers covering all areas of important issues. In addition, an annotated table of contents, an index, a book and periodical bibliography, and a list of organizations to contact are included in each book to expedite further research.

Perhaps more than ever before in history, people are confronted with diverse and contradictory information. During the Persian Gulf War, for example, the public was not only treated to minute-to-minute coverage of the war, it was also inundated with critiques of the coverage and countless analyses of the factors motivating U.S. involvement. Being able to sort through the plethora of opinions accompanying today's major issues, and to draw one's own conclusions, can be a complicated and frustrating struggle. It is the editors' hope that Current Controversies will help readers with this struggle.

Introduction

"The mechanism chosen by signatories of the Kyoto treaty for cutting global greenhouse gas emissions is called by a variety of names, among them carbon trading, emissions trading, cap-and-trade, and carbon offsets."

The majority of the world's scientists now believe that climate change is one of mankind's most urgent problems. According to a February 2007 report from the Intergovernmental Panel on Climate Change (IPCC), an entity created by the United Nations (UN) to examine the available evidence on the risk of human-induced climate change, global warming is "unequivocal" and has already resulted in rising temperatures, severe weather, rising sea levels, and melting glacier ice in the Arctic and Antarctic. The IPCC has urged the world to begin cutting greenhouse gas emissions immediately; and to achieve these cuts, the IPCC has endorsed the goals set forth in the Kyoto Protocol—an international agreement that set binding targets for the reduction of greenhouse gas emissions by thirty-seven industrialized countries and Europe. The Kyoto targets generally are set at an average of 5 percent reduction compared with 1990 levels for the five-year period of 2008 to 2012. Not all developed countries have signed the treaty, however. The United States, for example, has yet to sign the Kyoto Protocol or adopt a national emissions reduction goal.

The mechanism chosen by signatories of the Kyoto treaty for cutting global greenhouse gas emissions is called by a variety of names, among them carbon trading, emissions trading, cap-and-trade, and carbon offsets or credits. The basic idea is that governments, businesses, and other entities can compensate for their high carbon emissions by purchasing offsets or credits that pay for emissions-reducing activities elsewhere on the globe, often in less developed countries. By purchasing carbon or emissions credits or offsets, industrialized countries that otherwise might exceed their greenhouse gas emissions quotas under the Kyoto treaty can stay in compliance with Kyoto goals for overall global emission reductions.

In one type of emissions trading under Kyoto, sometimes referred to as "cap-and-trade," countries can earn carbon credits by reducing emissions below mandatory levels set by the Kyoto treaty. These credits can then be sold by one country to another country that has failed to meet its emissions targets. Similar trading of carbon credits can occur within each country. As an example, assume that a government has set an annual level of 100,000 tons of carbon dioxide emissions for each of two companies. If Company A successfully reduces its carbon emissions to 95,000 tons during a given year, but Company B fails to reduce emissions and produces 105,000 tons of emissions, Company A can then sell 5,000 tons of carbon credits to Company B. Under this scheme, both companies will have satisfied the government's requirements and, in theory, overall global carbon emissions will be reduced as required by the Kyoto treaty. This type of carbon trading is creating what is known as the carbon market, in which carbon emissions become a new type of marketable global commodity.

Other types of carbon trading programs authorized by Kyoto include the Clean Development Mechanism (CDM). CDM allows countries that have signed the Kyoto treaty to get credit for funding an emissions-reduction project in a developing country that is not part of the Kyoto scheme. Projects must be approved by a United Nations board and might involve, for example, rural electrification programs using solar panels or similar green technologies. Such projects can earn the implementing country one certified emission credit (CER) for each ton of carbon dioxide reduced. A similar program, called Joint Implementation (JI), allows Kyoto signatory countries to implement similar emissions reduction projects in countries that have signed the treaty. In these JI projects, the implementing country earns one emission reduction unit (ERU) for each ton of carbon dioxide that is reduced. Finally, Kyoto allows countries to earn removal units (RMUs) for funding land-use changes and so-called "carbon sink" projects, such as reforestation areas, that are believed to capture and absorb carbon dioxide from the atmosphere.

Alongside the carbon market set up under the mandates of the Kyoto treaty, however, there is a growing voluntary carbon market in countries that have not agreed to mandatory emissions cuts. Businesses and individuals in the United States, for example, have sought to purchase and trade carbon credits even in the absence of mandatory government requirements, simply because they want to help reduce global carbon emissions that contribute to global warming. Many believe that President Barack Obama will support a mandatory cap-and-trade scheme in the United States, and that the market created by such an action could produce a U.S. carbon market worth up to $1 trillion a year by 2020. Legislation also may begin to set some standards for carbon offset projects geared toward individual purchasers, but individuals will likely continue to have the option of voluntarily purchasing carbon credits or offsets from a variety of companies.

Carbon offsets, if effective, may hold the promise of helping to reduce overall global greenhouse gas emissions that are producing global warming, but a major debate has arisen concerning whether such offsets make any difference. Critics argue that many carbon credits are awarded for projects that would have been implemented anyway. Forestry projects are especially controversial, because tree-plantings are at best temporary carbon sinks and, in some cases, not environmentally friendly at all. Many see carbon offsets simply as a feel-good idea that allows people and companies in developed nations to believe they're doing something about global warming without having to actually change their behaviors or reduce their own emissions.

The viewpoints included in *Current Controversies: Carbon Offsets* reflect the various opinions and sides of this debate about carbon trading schemes, with chapters devoted to describing the current role of carbon offsets, whether they are effective in cutting greenhouse emissions, whether tree-related projects are beneficial, and how carbon offset programs can be improved to address current criticisms.

CHAPTER 1

How Do Carbon Offsets Work?

Chapter Overview

Mike Rosen-Molina

Mike Rosen-Molina is a writer and frequent contributor to The Monthly, *a general-interest regional magazine of culture and commerce for readers in the San Francisco Bay area.*

Although purchasing carbon credits (also referred to as "carbon offsets" in many circumstances) is a relatively new idea in the United States, it's gaining traction among green-minded consumers. . . . Many [people] don't see these credits as a blank check to be wasteful, but rather as an additional way to reduce emissions after making other lifestyle adjustments.

Al Gore, Ben & Jerry's ice cream, Clif Bar energy bars and The Barenaked Ladies rock band are just some of those investing in carbon offsets in order to reduce their gigantic carbon footprints. In 2007, the Academy Awards caused a stir by purchasing carbon credits to make up for the 250,000 pounds of carbon dioxide released during its annual ceremony. . . .

But as the concept gains popularity, it also gains critics who believe a system that doesn't yet enforce ceilings on greenhouse gas emissions—either on companies or individuals—is simply allowing people to buy an environmental indulgence. Some have cast carbon credits as an easy out for the rich and famous.

And in this new world of green-consciousness, consumers are asking tough questions: Does this really reduce carbon in the environment or just make us feel better? Who is monitoring these offsets? How do we know that the net result is really carbon neutral? And will the ability to trade carbon credits mean that individuals (especially those with the means) and

Mike Rosen-Molina, "Carbon Credit Report: Can Buying Carbon Credits to Offset the Greenhouse Gases You Spew in Daily Life Really Help Save Us from Global Warming?" *The Monthly*, vol. 37, August 2007. www.themonthly.com. Reproduced by permission.

corporations alike will keep on using what they're using and simply buy their way out of any pinch related to "reduce, reuse and recycle?"

The idea of carbon trading really took off in the Kyoto Protocol, a 1997 international agreement between 169 countries to reduce greenhouse gases.

What Is Carbon Trading?

Carbon credits seem at once deceptively simple and completely baffling, part of a larger emerging system called "the carbon market." Here's how it works: the government sets a limit on how much carbon dioxide a factory can spew into the atmosphere. Because the onus to comply is on factory owners not to exceed that limit, ostensibly they will do everything that's cost-effective to mitigate their pollution. That may mean buying new, more energy-efficient equipment or looking into alternative fuel sources like wind or solar power. Even so, the company may come in 100 tons over quota. In that case, it can invest in a carbon offset—in essence, a promise that somewhere, someone else will pollute 100 tons less carbon. The factory might still be releasing too much carbon dioxide, but the net result is "carbon neutrality" as some other factory slows down its own carbon dioxide output.

[California] is the first in the nation to place caps on industries in order to reduce carbon dioxide.

The idea of carbon trading really took off in the Kyoto Protocol, a 1997 international agreement between 169 countries to reduce greenhouse gases. The treaty set up a system wherein member states could trade credits to one another to meet treaty-established quotas for the reduction of greenhouse emissions. One credit is considered equivalent to one ton of carbon dioxide emissions.

Many advocates expect that it's only a matter of time until the United States joins this effort and begins to regulate the carbon dioxide output of its industries. Until then, there's just California.

Under California's landmark AB32, the state is the first in the nation to place caps on industries in order to reduce carbon dioxide. The law will require the state to reduce its greenhouse gas emissions to 1990 levels by 2020. In order to do so, California must first determine the baseline 1990 level and then implement a plan that places hard caps on utilities and industries to incrementally reduce greenhouse gas output. California companies will be given "allowances" for how much they can emit and eventually trade those with each other.

City governments and individuals aren't held to any carbon caps—not yet—but can participate in a voluntary carbon market.

Individuals can also purchase credits from several local and national companies that have emerged over the past few years.

Across the country, cities like Berkeley and Oakland are joining the Chicago Climate Exchange (CCX), a voluntary, legally binding greenhouse gas reduction and trading system for emission sources and offset projects in North America. Timothy Burroughs, climate action coordinator for Berkeley, says the city government has consistently reduced emissions related to its operations annually and earned credits on the Chicago exchange. But instead of selling those credits, Berkeley has chosen to retire them—a net positive for the environment.

"If we are urging our community to reduce its carbon footprint, then we certainly have to be doing it ourselves,"

Burroughs says. "We're providing an example for our own community members but also for other cities.". . .

Individuals can also purchase credits from several local and national companies that have emerged over the past few years. For an annual fee ranging from $40 to $100, the Bay Area's TerraPass will fund eco-projects to counterbalance carbon generated by driving a car. Native Energy in Vermont can invest your money to build new wind farms and biomass projects.

Getting Your Money's Worth

It sounds like a good cause, but what does this all mean? For many laypeople, the world of carbon trading is a jungle of technical jargon. And when you're paying for something that you can't see or touch, it's sometimes hard to be sure you're getting your money's worth.

According to experts, there's a lot to consider, but two of the big issues in determining the good done by a credit are "additionality" and "leakage."

The concept of additionality holds that the money poured into carbon offsets has to actually make a difference—it has to create some benefit that, absent that contribution, never would have come to fruition. In other words, a company has to actively reduce its carbon output for you to be able to buy it as a legitimate credit.

Now the concept gets complicated. An eco-conscious company that builds a new factory that uses biomass and renewable energy would not be eligible for carbon offset funding because the money put in wouldn't cause any "additional" reduction in carbon dioxide. But a developing country that produces needed electricity with an antiquated, polluting factory would be the perfect candidate. If an investor contributed money to finance a greener plant, here there would be "additionality"—an additional reduction in carbon dioxide that would not have existed without that money.

"The Kyoto Protocol set up the additionality requirement because they didn't want to just credit people for doing business as usual," says Tom Kelly, cofounder of KyotoUSA, a grassroots organization that works to encourage cities and local groups nationwide to reduce greenhouse gases for which they are responsible. "They really have to go above and beyond to reduce carbon. This is part of what makes carbon offsets such a difficult area, because it's so hard to identify and measure what's truly a credit."

In short, a good offset should have additionality and shouldn't have leakage.

The second factor, "leakage," is easier to understand but almost as difficult to measure.

"You might decide to protect a certain tract of forest that wouldn't otherwise be protected," explains Laura Harnish, deputy regional director of Environmental Defense, one of the nation's largest environmental organizations. "But then if some other forest is harvested instead—one that would have been left standing—you've got leakage."

In short, a good offset should have additionality and shouldn't have leakage.

Some consumers view carbon offsets as tools for awareness and even a bandage, but not the cure-all.

Differing Views About Carbon Credits

Even with solid analysis about the ins and outs of what makes a good carbon credit, some consumers view carbon offsets as tools for awareness and even a bandage, but not the cure-all. Others have a dimmer view.

"That's a crock," says Hank Chapot, 52, a gardener on the U.C. Berkeley campus who takes his environmentally friendly lifestyle very seriously. "They tell you that you can buy carbon credits so that you'll feel good and then they claim that they'll invest into alternative fuel sources, but it's a feel-good scam. I can say that I've bought 200 acres of biomass farm or 200 megawatts of wind power so I can feel good about my next air trip."

One of Chapot's main complaints is that a carbon market will reward the large corporations that are historic polluters—the oil and energy companies—by awarding them credits to trade. At the same time, he says, carbon trading is a one-way street for ordinary people: You can buy a credit to counteract your car exhaust, but if you're a regular Joe who rides a bike to work, you don't get any credits to sell.

[Some people] criticize carbon trading as encouraging business as usual, allowing corporations or individuals to buy their way out of cleaning up their acts.

Chapot, who doesn't own a car, bikes to work in the morning. When he does need to drive, he borrows a car from City CarShare, something that he estimates he's done only about 10 times in the last year. He chooses locally grown foods when he shops at the Berkeley Bowl, avoiding produce that had to travel long distances in carbon-spouting trucks to get to grocery store shelves. Although he understands that not everyone is capable of living a low-carbon lifestyle, he still thinks that there are better solutions than buying carbon credits.

Chapot and others criticize carbon trading as encouraging business as usual, allowing corporations or individuals to buy their way out of cleaning up their acts.

"The best solution is to just stop doing it," says Chapot. "Don't sign up for carbon credits, just stop burning carbon. Wear a sweater in the winter instead of cranking up the heat.

Quit buying bottled water. Bike to work or use public transportation. There are plenty of low-tech ways to solve the problem."

Carbon Credit Sellers

Across the country, numerous companies have opened their doors to sell credits to eco-conscious consumers—often at wildly different prices for what seems, at first glance, to be the same thing. But carbon retailers will tell you that subtle differences exist between the credits sold by different competitors, depending on how those credits are generated.

"Some marketers like to commoditize carbon with the mantra, 'A ton is a ton is a ton,'" says Billy Connelly, marketing director for Native Energy, a Vermont-based carbon-trading company that sells credits to businesses and individuals. Native Energy credits cost more than other credits, explains Connelly, because they are like "gourmet credits." The company works only with start-ups, rather than buying and selling credits on the market. The company's direct relationship with projects makes it easier to monitor how much carbon dioxide is displaced.

"Many other markets just buy energy credits from the 'super market,' so you don't really know what you're getting," says Connelly.

Customers who have bought credits from Native Energy include Ben & Jerry's ice cream, Green Mountain Coffee Roasters and the band R.E.M.

Bay Area-based TerraPass buys and retires credits from the Chicago Climate Exchange, but also invests in clean energy through wind farms and biomass.

TerraPass prides itself on stopping methane (a greenhouse gas that causes even more damage than carbon dioxide) from getting into the atmosphere by "methane capture" on dairy farms. (Yes, that means removing the gas produced by farm animals.) Among its customers are Ford Motors, which purchased credits to offset carbon dioxide created during the construction of its hybrid car fleet, and the Academy Awards. TerraPass has recently partnered with Washington, D.C.-based FlexCar, giving FlexCar customers across the country the option of purchasing credits for the miles they drive.

TerraPass is also unique in its commitment to "match maturity"—meaning that all the credits you buy result in real carbon reductions within the year.

"For example, if you buy a credit for 10 tons of carbon that's reduced by a reforestation project, it might take 100 years for the trees to take up that 10 tons," says Tom Arnold, chief environmental officer at TerraPass. "We don't think we have that kind of time, so all TerraPass projects offset the carbon the same year that you buy the credit."

Both TerraPass and Native Energy, like the majority of carbon-trading companies, are privately-owned, for-profit corporations, something that may give potential buyers pause. But since carbon offsets are bought and sold as commodities on a market, companies say the for-profit model gives them a better ability to buy and sell within that context.

The U.S. carbon market is a confusing free-for-all.

"Energy is a for-profit business," says Arnold. "There are no nonprofit farmers or wind farms. These are the businesses that are going to make a difference in reducing carbon, and it's all profit-driven. You have to set up incentives for businesses to do the right thing."

Billy Connelly agrees that the for-profit model has its role to play.

"Many consumers think that environmental stewardship is the realm of the nonprofit," says Connelly. "But without the discipline of the bottom line, we wouldn't be able to gauge our success. This makes us better equipped to compete with other for-profit corporations because you have to be competitive."

Problems in the Voluntary Carbon Market

Overseas, carbon trading is a heavily regulated industry in nations that have signed on to the Kyoto Protocol, but there's little government oversight for the industry in the United States. As a result, the U.S. carbon market is a confusing free-for-all, where scholars, advocates and trading companies often disagree on what, exactly, qualifies as a credit and how to measure its value. Environmental-minded consumers are often left without any way of knowing what they're really buying.

"The voluntary carbon market has been referred to as the wild, wild West," says Caitlin Sparks, U.S. marketing representative for The Gold Standard. The Gold Standard is an independent nonprofit that has developed a set of voluntary guidelines for carbon offset projects to ensure that carbon credits achieve real emissions reductions. "The market is entirely unregulated and lacks federal legislation and guidelines. Consequently, it's hard for buyers to know what they are actually purchasing. Many credit retailers have been widely criticized for offering credits that don't achieve any real, measurable reductions."

Companies that sell carbon credits also have vastly different business models. Some function as little more than middlemen—buying up credits and selling them at a markup. That model has been criticized for making it hard to tell where the credits originally come from. Other companies work with projects from scratch to ensure that the credits they generate are on the level.

"The major problems are with standards and oversight. Consumers don't know what they're getting," says Connelly. "It's also very complicated, and not yet a well known service. It's not like gumballs. When you buy a gumball, you can tell a lot by looking at it. You can tell the difference between a good and bad gumball, a big and a small one, blue and red, but carbon offsets are so complex that people start to glaze over when they have to hear about the differences between different ones."

Kelly of KyotoUSA [a group urging U.S. cities to reduce carbon emissions] agrees that the checks and balances aren't in place yet.

"Because we're unregulated and because we live in a capitalist economy and because a lot of people are concerned about climate change, companies will sell them these credits," says Kelly. "But if you try to follow the money trail, it's often difficult to tell how much of your money goes for that purpose."

Carbon Trading Is a U.S.-Proposed Market Solution for Global Climate Change

Larry Lohmann

Larry Lohmann works with Corner House, a nongovernmental research organization based in the United Kingdom.

Corporations, academics, governments, United Nations [UN] agencies and environmentalists [have] united around a neoliberal or 'market' approach to climate change emanating from North America. . . .

The Market Fix

The . . . strategy for containing the political threats implied by climate change—while at the same time using it to create new opportunities for corporate profit—is the 'market fix'.

The . . . strategy for containing the political threats implied by climate change . . . is the 'market fix'.

The market fix began to take shape in the late 1980s and early 1990s. Public pressure was growing for governments to agree to do something about global warming. Some of the changes needed had been obvious since the 1970s. These included long-term shifts in the structure of Northern industrial, transport and household energy use away from wasteful expenditure of fossil fuels toward frugal use of solar and other renewable sources. Tackling the problem internationally meant addressing the institutions and power imbalances that had re-

"Carbon Trading: A Critical Conversation on Climate Change, Privatisation and Power," *Development Dialogue*, Vol. 48, special issue, edited by Larry Lohmann, September 2006, pp. 31, 45–46, 48, 50–51, 63. www.dhf.uu.se. Reproduced by permission.

sulted in both the overuse and the globally unequal use of the earth's carbon-absorbing capacity.

That sort of action would have been hard for corporations, governments and UN agencies to accept unless they were under a lot of public pressure to do so. . . . It also required a historical and political perspective unfamiliar to many climate scientists and technocrats. It was easier to view global warming's causes in simple physical terms—'too much greenhouse gas'—without looking too carefully at what would have to be done to tackle the problem. The priority became to set some targets while leaving the 'how' of long-term structural change for later.

[The market approach to climate change] was 'made in the USA.'

Many international negotiators and their advisers were encouraged to take this approach by the precedent of the 1987 Montreal Protocol on Substances that Deplete the Ozone Layer. The Montreal agreement had been a technocrat's dream. Spearheaded by Northern scientific bureaucracies and governments, it had never had to scrutinise the industrial system as a whole. The ozone problem was presented as nothing more than 'flights of inanimate particles from activities deemed benign in themselves, and not the lifestyles of the rich and famous', to quote the wry assessment of Harvard's Sheila Jasanoff.

But the treaty worked. Unlike global warming, the ozone problem didn't require long-term restructuring of energy sectors central to industrialised economies. Only a few factories were involved. It was relatively easy to set a target and find substitutes for some ozone-depleting substances or phase them out. With the eventual backing of industry itself and the help of a few transition-aiding payments to Southern [less developed] nations, nearly all nations wound up complying with the agreement. . . .

Many climate negotiators thought a similar idea might work with global warming. They were even guided by some of the same scientist-bureaucrats. Targets and timetables for reducing emissions became the big issue. Few questions were asked about power, property, and path-dependence.

Into this vacuum rushed the idea that the technical means of achieving reductions could best be left to the private sector and 'technology transfer'. And if corporations were going to be the stars of the show, why not make it as cheap and profitable as possible for them to meet whatever targets had been set?. . .

The pollution-trading mechanisms that formed the core of the Kyoto Protocol were of a type proposed by North American economists in the 1960s [for air pollutants].

This was the market fix. . . . The earth's carbon dump would gradually be made economically scarce through limits on its use imposed by states. Tradeable legal rights to it would be created and distributed to the biggest emitters. Bargaining would generate a price that would reflect the value society (that is, governments) placed on carbon dump use. Emitters who found ways of using the dump more efficiently could profit by selling their unused rights to more backward producers. They could also develop new dumps. The market would 'help society find and move along the least-cost pollution reduction supply curve'.

As Michael Zammit Cutajar, the former executive secretary of the UNFCCC [United Nations Framework Convention on Climate Change, a 1992 international treaty on climate change] has stressed, this approach was 'made in the USA'. The pollution-trading mechanisms that formed the core of the Kyoto Protocol [an international agreement to reduce greenhouse gas emissions] were of a type proposed by North American economists in the 1960s; put into practice in US markets for lead, nitrogen oxides and sulphur dioxide and other pollutants beginning in the 1970s and 1980s; and successfully pressed on the UN by the US government, advised by US economists, US NGOs [nongovernmental organizations] and US business, in the 1990s. . . .

The Success of the Market Fix

Why was US pressure to turn the Kyoto Protocol into a set of market mechanisms so successful? There's no simple answer. Almost certainly, many factors were involved.

First, there is sheer force of numbers. In the 2000 UN-FCCC climate negotiations in The Hague, to take one example, the US fielded 150 well-equipped delegates, housing them in a luxury hotel and sending well-rested and well-briefed representatives to every working group meeting, while Mozambique had to put up its three harried delegates in a noisy youth hostel occupied largely by Chinese tourists. During complex negotiations featuring many simultaneous sessions and drafts of hundreds of crucial documents flying around for continuous comment and revision, such numerical superiority can be decisive.

Most countries had neither the background nor the staff to . . . counter, or even understand, a complicated pollution-trading policy.

The US was also able to impose a language on the climate talks in which objections to neoliberal policies could not be effectively made. As IPCC [Intergovernmental Panel on Climate Change, a panel set up by the United Nations in 1988 to study climate change] member Wolfgang Sachs notes, orthodox economics and public policy methodology prevented the question even being raised as to what type of changes would be necessary to reduce greenhouse gas concentrations to a safer level or allocate atmospheric rights equitably. Officials of most countries had neither the background nor the staff to work out in time how to counter, or even to understand, a complicated pollution-trading policy jargon essentially 'made in the USA'.

In addition, the structure of the climate negotiations was itself biased in favour of US interests. As scholar Joyeeta Gupta notes, standard UN negotiating techniques such as 'avoiding polarisation', 'incrementally building on agreement', and pretending to be guided by international legal norms handicap activist Southern diplomats by automatically relegating talk of structural change to the category of the 'merely rhetorical' or 'irrelevant'. Privately, too, negotiators also often speak of US trade threats, bribes and 'dirty tricks', although diplomats and other officials who are successfully targeted often want to keep the news off the record as much as the US itself does.

One example of US influence in the negotiations comes from the Kyoto Protocol talks themselves. In 1997 Brazil proposed a 'Clean Development Fund' that would use penalties paid by industrialised countries that had exceeded their emissions targets to finance 'no regrets' clean energy initiatives in the South.

The structure of the climate negotiations was itself biased in favour of US interests.

The gist of Brazil's proposal was accepted by the G-77 nations [also known as the Group of 77 at the United Nations, the G-77 is a loose coalition of developing nations designed to promote its members collective economic interests] and China. During a few days of intense negotiations, however, the fund was transformed into a trading mechanism allowing industrialised countries to buy rights to pollute from countries with no emissions limits. Fines were transformed into prices; a judicial system was transformed into a market.

How? Smaller negotiating groups assigned to discuss channelling penalties for Northern failure to meet emissions targets to a fund for the South were dominated by Northern delegates who wanted to dodge the issue of penalties as much as possible. The 'direct link between compliance and the fund dissolved' and the negotiations turned into a gruelling series of sessions on how to convert the clean development fund into a version of a trading scheme the US had already been backing. . . .

The Clean Development Mechanism [a type of carbon trading adopted by the Kyoto Protocol] that resulted now occupies an immense slice of UN time and involves billion-dollar money flows despite the fact that its effect on the climate may well be negative. . . .

Carbon Trading—An Accepted Agenda

A market fix . . . [has now] come to be intertwined in climate change politics in an intimate way.

The recent US neoliberal innovation known as the pollution market, growing largely out of academic theory, NGO advocacy and an anti-regulation backlash among corporations, moved with startling speed into international climate politics in the 1990s. Fed by a corporate-friendly reading of climate science and economics, as well as research into technological fixes, it drew UN agencies and activists alike into its gravitational field, eventually triumphing over early Southern [that is, the developing world] and European opposition through complex and still partly obscure political processes. An astonishing range of institutions from private companies to UN agencies, university departments and NGOs are now aligned around an agenda characterised by rejection of precaution, inability to come to terms with indeterminacy and irreversibility, insistence that tradeoffs are always possible, and support for growth in corporate power. . . .

[In the] debate [about climate change] . . . the only questions spoken are the narrow ones large corporations most want to hear. Is there or is there not human-caused climate change? If there is, what might make continued fossil fuel use possible? How can more subsidies be channelled to technologies corporations can profit from? How can privatisation and 'efficiency' be furthered in a way most acceptable to the public? Such questions are uniting the most cynical corporate hack and the most innocent environmental activist in a single agenda.

The European Union Is a Pioneer in Carbon Trading

Eileen Claussen

Eileen Claussen is the President of the Pew Center on Global Climate Change and Strategies for the Global Environment. Claussen is the former Assistant Secretary of State for Oceans and International Environmental and Scientific Affairs.

To meet its obligations to reduce greenhouse gas (GHG) concentrations under the Kyoto Protocol, the European Union (EU) established the first cap-and-trade system for carbon dioxide emissions in the world starting in 2005. Proposed in October 2001, the EU's Emissions Trading System (EU ETS) was up and running just over three years later. The first three-year trading period (2005–2007)—a trial period before Kyoto's obligations began—is now complete and, not surprisingly, has been heavily scrutinized. This report examines the development, structure, and performance of the EU ETS to date, and provides insightful analysis regarding the controversies and lessons emerging from the initial trial phase.

Recognizing their lack of experience with cap-and-trade and the need to build knowledge and program architecture, EU leaders began by covering only one gas (carbon dioxide) and a limited number of sectors. Once the infrastructure was in place, other GHGs and sectors could be included in subsequent phases of the program, when more significant emissions reductions were needed. As authors Denny Ellerman and Paul Joskow describe, the system has so far worked as it was envisioned—a European-wide carbon price was established, businesses began incorporating this price into their decision-making, and the market infrastructure for a multi-national

Eileen Claussen, "Foreword, Executive Summary," *The European Union's Emission Trading System in Perspective*, by A. Denny Ellerman and Paul L. Joskow, PEW Center on Global Climate Change, May 2008. www.pewclimate.org. Reproduced by permission.

trading program is now in place. Moreover, despite the condensed time period of the trial phase, some reductions in emissions from the covered sectors were realized.

The development of the EU ETS [emissions trading system] has not, however, proceeded without its challenges.

Performance of the EU ETS

The development of the EU ETS has not, however, proceeded without its challenges. . . .

The performance of the European Union's Emissions Trading System (EU ETS) to date cannot be evaluated without recognizing that the first three years from 2005 through 2007 constituted a "trial" period and understanding what this trial period was supposed to accomplish. Its primary goal was to develop the infrastructure and to provide the experience that would enable the successful use of a cap-and-trade system to limit European GHG emissions during a second trading period, 2008–12, corresponding to the first commitment period of the Kyoto Protocol. The trial period was a rehearsal for the later more serious engagement and it was never intended to achieve significant reductions in CO_2 emissions in only three years. In light of the speed with which the program was developed, the many sovereign countries involved, the need to develop the necessary data, information dissemination, compliance and market institutions, and the lack of extensive experience with emissions trading in Europe, we think that the system has performed surprisingly well.

A significant segment of European industry is incorporating the price of CO_2 emissions into their daily production decisions.

Although there have been plenty of rough edges, a transparent and widely accepted price for tradable CO_2 emission allowances emerged by January 1, 2005, a functioning market for allowances has developed quickly and effortlessly without any prodding by the Commission or member state governments, the cap-and-trade infrastructure of market institutions, registries, monitoring, reporting and verification is in place, and a significant segment of European industry is incorporating the price of CO_2 emissions into their daily production decisions.

Lessons for the Future

The development of the EU ETS and the experience with the trial period provides a number of useful lessons for the U.S. and other countries.

- Suppliers quickly factor the price of emissions allowances into their pricing and output behavior.

- Liquid bilateral markets and public allowance exchanges emerge rapidly and the "law of one price" for allowances with the same attributes prevails.

- The development of efficient allowance markets is facilitated by the frequent dissemination of information about emissions and allowance utilization.

- Allowance price volatility can be dampened by including allowance banking and borrowing and by allocating allowances for longer trading periods.

- The redistributive aspects of the allocation process can be handled without distorting abatement efficiency or competition despite the significant political maneuvering over allowance allocations. However, allocations that are tied to future emissions through investment and closure decisions can distort behavior.

- The interaction between allowance allocation, allowance markets, and the unsettled state of electricity sector liberalization and regulation must be confronted as part of program design to avoid mistakes and unintended consequences. This will be especially important in the U.S. where 50 percent of the electricity is generated with coal.

A Global System of Carbon Trading

The EU ETS provides a useful perspective on the problems to be faced in constructing a global GHG emission trading system. In imagining a multinational system, it seems clear that participating nations will retain significant discretion in deciding tradable national emission caps albeit with some negotiation; separate national registries will be maintained with some arrangement for international transfers; and monitoring, reporting and verification procedures will be administered nationally although necessarily subject to some common standard. All of these issues have had to be addressed in the trial period and they continue to present challenges to European policy makers.

The deeper significance of the trial period of the EU ETS may be its explicit status as a work in progress. As such, it is emblematic of all climate change programs, which will surely be changed over the long horizon during which they will remain effective. The trial period demonstrates that everything does not need to be perfect at the beginning. In fact, it provides a reminder that the best can be the enemy of the good. This admonition is especially applicable in an imperfect world where the income and wealth effects of proposed actions are significant and sovereign nations of widely varying economic circumstance and institutional development are involved. The initial challenge is simply to establish a system that will demonstrate the societal decision that GHG emissions shall have a price and to provide the signal of what constitutes appropriate short-term and long-term measures to limit GHG emissions.

In this, the EU has done more with the ETS, despite all its faults, than any other nation or set of nations.

The United States Is Poised to Create Its Own Mandatory Carbon Trading Program

Bob Keefe

Bob Keefe is a national correspondent for Cox Newspapers based in Southern California.

What's the price of pollution?

Soon, the greenhouse gases that big companies produce may be priced, sold and traded just like shares of stock, creating a whole new industry in the United States that could dramatically affect the national economy.

Building on current laws addressing acid rain and smog, Congress [soon] . . . could vote on a national "cap-and-trade" system that would limit carbon emissions by big companies. Under such systems, the amount of allowable gases from each producer is capped, and those who produce more or less can buy or sell each other carbon "credits."

[President Barack Obama] will likely support such a plan. . . .

Voluntary Efforts

Some parts of the country aren't waiting on Washington.

In the Northeast, power plants in 10 states will face regional carbon cap-and-trade rules beginning next year. In California, a more extensive system could affect virtually all businesses starting in 2012. Other states are watching California closely.

Bob Keefe, "Some See a 'Tidal Wave' of Carbon Trading in Nation's Future," *Atlanta Journal Constitution*, Living Green, February 29, 2008. www.ajc.com. Republished with permission of Atlanta Journal Constitution, conveyed through Copyright Clearance Center, Inc.

Europe already has an extensive carbon cap-and-trade market that's now being expanded.

"You don't even have to believe all this climate change stuff, you just have to believe that all the politicians believe it," said Henry Derwent, CEO of the International Emissions Trading Association. "And if that's right, the carbon restraints are just going to keep on coming."

Already, many companies—Dell Inc., Nike Inc. and Atlanta-based flooring maker Interface Inc., to name a few—have voluntarily agreed to go "carbon neutral" in part because it's the right thing to do, but also for public relations purposes and to get ahead of any forthcoming regulations.

Cities such as Austin, Texas, also have pledged to make their municipal operations "carbon neutral" in coming years. Atlanta and other cities have promised to build only carbon-neutral buildings in the future.

Despite the growth of the voluntary market, mandatory carbon regulations would dramatically change the business of pollution.

Generally, those who voluntarily reduce their carbon "footprints" both cut their own emissions and buy "carbon offsets," such as helping fund programs like tree planting or building renewable energy plants in developing countries.

Five years ago, a former Chicago Board of Trade economist even set up North America's first trading system for companies that want to buy, sell or trade contracts for voluntary carbon emissions. The Chicago Climate Exchange now works with more than 300 companies.

A Tidal Wave

But despite the growth of the voluntary market, mandatory carbon regulations would dramatically change the business of pollution.

"I don't think it's going to be a ripple, it's going to be a tidal wave" if the United States starts a cap-and-trade system, said Dirk Forrister(cq), managing director of carbon consulting firm NatSource.

If Europe is any indication, such a system in the U.S. would create a huge new industry for carbon monitoring, trading and consulting. It could help spur more energy innovation and boost the potential of the growing number of "clean tech" companies.

In an indication of just how big the pollution business could become, more than 1,400 attendees converged here [San Francisco] last week [February 2008] for a first-of-its-kind Carbon Forum America sponsored by Derwent's organization [International Emissions Trading Association]. A separate event drew venture capitalists and clean tech companies.

"A cap-and-trade system will not only significantly reduce our nation's carbon footprint, it also will generate tremendous economic activity (and create) a whole new green economy," Sen. Dianne Feinstein, D-Calif., said in a videotaped statement opening the forum.

Some [environmentalists] worry that letting companies buy carbon credits will let them delay reducing their own emissions.

Pros and Cons of Carbon Trading

Or, according to opponents, it could devastate the U.S. economy.

The U.S. Chamber of Commerce claims that if the America's Climate Security Act offered by Sens. Joseph Lieberman, a Connecticut independent, and John Warner, R-Va., becomes law, 3.4 million Americans could lose their jobs and the gross domestic product will decline by $1 trillion.

Video ads running on the business advocacy group's Web site portray American families sleeping in sweaters, cooking with candles and jogging to work in the future because of high electricity costs.

Some congressional allies of business are also opposed. House Republican leader John Boehner of Ohio last month [January 2008] ridiculed Speaker Nancy Pelosi's "Green the Capitol" program of purchasing carbon offsets as a "waste of money."

Even environmental groups have doubts about cap and trade. Some worry that letting companies buy carbon credits will let them delay reducing their own emissions.

Some utilities support the idea of a national [carbon trading] program . . . but others say the . . . proposal would drive up power prices dramatically.

Utilities would be most affected by carbon cap-and-trade rules, because they're the biggest emitters of greenhouse gases. Some utilities support the idea of a national program instead of state-by-state regulations, but others say the Lieberman-Warner proposal would drive up power prices dramatically—especially in the Southeast and Midwest, which are most dependent on coal-fired power plants.

"Obviously we are opposed to the Lieberman-Warner bill," said Valerie Holpp, spokeswoman for Atlanta-based energy company Southern Co. More than 70 percent of the company's power plants throughout the Southeast are coal-fired.

Holpp said the bill's proposal to cut the nation's greenhouse gas emissions by 19 percent (from 2005 levels) by 2020 and 63 percent by 2050 are unachievable with present technology.

Charlotte, N.C.-based Duke Energy says it supports carbon reduction plans, but not the Lieberman-Warner proposal, specifically because it would require power companies to buy carbon credits through an auction system.

"Having to obtain allowances for existing coal plants through an auction is nothing more than a carbon tax," Duke Energy Chairman Jim Rogers said in a statement. "It should be called what it is—a disproportionate tax on consumers in the 25 states that depend on coal."

Even so, many businesses support new regulations on greenhouse gas emissions. Last year, some of the nation's biggest companies—including Juno Beach, Fla.-based FPL Group, Alcoa, BP America, Duke Energy, Dow Chemical and carmakers Ford, GM and Chrysler—created a business group to support a carbon cap-and-trade system.

Some businesses see potential profits in selling or trading credits.

They also expect that participating can help them look better in the eyes of investors and customers, who increasingly consider greenhouse gas emissions a business liability. It also can help businesses level the environmental playing field with competitors.

Some say companies also are realizing that cutting carbon emissions is simply inevitable.

More of them are seeing "they'll have to take on the price of carbon in one way or another in the very near future," said Jonathan Shopley, executive director of the CarbonNetural Co., a consulting firm that sells carbon offsets in Europe. "They also know that early action has real benefits."

Carbon Offsets Are Now the Cornerstone of International Efforts to Slow Global Warming

Renfrey Clarke

Renfrey Clarke is an Australian school teacher, writer, and a correspondent for progressive news sources.

Amid audible gasps of relief, on December 15 [2007] the US delegation to the United Nations climate change conference in Bali [Indonesia] signalled that Washington would be part of the "Bali Roadmap" for combatting global warming. With the US on board, a two-year process of discussion would begin—hopefully to culminate in the adoption of a new pact to replace the Kyoto Protocol [an international agreement to cut greenhouse gas emissions], due to expire in 2012.

But no-one was breaking out the champagne. The US consent had come at an ominous price. Time-frames had been left vague or non-existent. Negotiators for US President George [W.] Bush's administration had forced any specific targets for emission cuts to be dropped from the roadmap. The point had been rammed home that any international pact that grew from the Bali conference would depend strictly on Washington's readiness to accept its provisions.

And well before the tense, drawn-out final session at Bali, it had emerged that the shambolic system of international carbon emissions trading set up on the basis of decisions taken at Kyoto in 1997 would remain. Moreover, the system had been given a new reach into the Third World. Carbon trading had been accepted as one of the cornerstones of a new adap-

Renfrey Clarke, "Bali Climate Conference Reaffirms Carbon Trading Scam," *Green Left Online*, vol. 737, January 30, 2008. Reproduced by permission of *Green Left Weekly*, www.greenleft.org.au.

tation fund, meant supposedly to help poor countries deal with the effects of global warming.

Carbon trading [has] . . . been accepted as one of the cornerstones of a new adaptation fund, . . . to help poor countries deal with the effects of global warming.

If these countries wanted help from the fund, it was made plain, they would have to pay for it by surrendering large elements of their national sovereignty. In particular, natural assets such as forests would have to be opened to the operations of the world emissions market.

In the words of an NGO [nongovernmental organization] delegate quoted by writer Brian Tokar, the Bali conference had been turned into "a giant shopping extravaganza, marketing the earth, the sky and the rights of the poor".

Carbon trading is to extend far beyond mere country-to-country adjustments to become a worldwide system of emissions-related investment.

Cap and Trade

The commercial mechanism put in place by the Kyoto Protocol is known as "cap and trade". Setting the goal of reducing developed-country emissions to 5.2% below 1990 levels by 2012, the system assigns an emissions "cap", consisting of a certain number of tonnes per year of "carbon dioxide equivalent", to participating states. If countries manage to keep their emissions below this permitted level, they have the right to sell "carbon credits" corresponding to these savings to other countries that exceed their caps.

Over time, the plan is to reduce the size of the caps, increasing the scarcity and raising the price of carbon credits. In theory, emitters will respond to these cost pressures by changing their practices and cutting their emissions.

As projected by its enthusiasts, carbon trading is to extend far beyond mere country-to-country adjustments to become a worldwide system of emissions-related investment. As well as being rewarded for setting up greenhouse gas-reducing projects elsewhere in the industrialised world, developed-country governments and corporations are to receive credits for undertaking emissions reduction or avoidance projects in underdeveloped countries.

"Win-Win" Outcomes?

In theory, the scheme promotes "win-win" outcomes for all involved. But the officials who set it up reckoned without the fact that in capitalism, the all-important bottom line measures profits, not environmental benefits. In practice, corporations have regularly found it cheaper to sidestep the new system or to subvert its purpose rather than to join in saving the planet.

The only large-scale carbon trading program yet to be initiated under the Kyoto Protocol is the European Union Emissions Trading Scheme (EU ETS).

The only large-scale carbon trading program yet to be initiated under the Kyoto Protocol is the European Union Emissions Trading Scheme (EU ETS), which began functioning in January 2005. In the program's first phase, emissions licences were "grandfathered"—that is, granted free of charge to established corporations. With little independent information, the people administering the scheme were often forced to rely on emissions estimates prepared by the firms themselves. Needless to say, these figures gave the corporations generous leeway.

Add in corporate lobbying and the result was massive over-allocation of emissions permits, which in some areas of industry exceeded actual emissions by as much as 50%. In

May 2006, after the scale of this over-allocation burst into the open, the market in carbon credits collapsed.

When the "right to pollute" can be had so cheaply, investing money in cutting emissions becomes irrational behavior.

For European companies to have sufficient incentives to actually reduce their emissions, estimates hold, the price of carbon credits needs to be in the range of 30 to 50 euros (A$50–85). But in the period since the crash, the market price of these credits has regularly fallen below one euro. When the "right to pollute" can be had so cheaply, investing money in cutting emissions becomes irrational behaviour.

Subsequent emissions trading schemes, pro-market commentators assure us, will avoid such fiascos. Instead of emissions permits being handed out gratis when schemes are launched, these licences will be sold at auction. But the enthusiasts for cap-and-trade systems forget another propensity of the corporate world: for corruption.

Even if carbon credits retail for not much more than a dollar each, they are good business if they can be created for almost nothing. Perhaps the easiest way to create them cheaply is to claim them for changes that were going to be made anyway.

Deciding whether such changes are genuinely "additional"—that is, made primarily in order to reduce emissions—can be extremely difficult. In the Third World, with its weak state bodies and ill-paid officials, the openings for malfeasance are endless. "It's routine practice for Indian project developers to fake documents, for example back-dating board approval, that they considered a project on the basis of the Kyoto Protocol", one former UN [United Nations] adviser acknowledged.

Scandals and Rorts

Some of the sharpest practice, technically speaking, has not been illegal at all. British science writer George Monblot described one such manoeuvre: "Entrepreneurs in India and China have made billions by building factories whose primary purpose is to produce greenhouse gases, so that carbon traders in the rich world will pay to clean them up."

In 2006, according to the World Bank, 64% of the emissions credits traded came from changes in the refrigerant industry—above all, from reduced emissions by Chinese and Indian refrigerant plants of a gas known as HFC-23. This gas has a greenhouse potential no less than 11,700 times that of carbon dioxide.

For the industrialists who have cut back on emitting it, the journal *Nature* revealed last year [2007], HFC-23 has so far yielded some US$5.9 billion. Meanwhile, the total worldwide cost of installing chemical scrubbers to halt emissions of the gas—something that could readily be compelled by environmental laws—would not be much more than $100 million.

In practice, the [Bali] adaptation fund is likely to act as a tool for taking control of important natural assets of poor countries.

While the opportunities for rorting the Kyoto system have been a boon to Third World elites—or at least, to their more crooked members—the system as a whole does not promise well for underdeveloped countries. The new adaptation fund set up at the Bali conference, it turns out, is to be administered by the Global Environmental Facility of the World Bank. In its lending for development projects, the World Bank is notorious for favouring schemes that lock the economies of poor countries into the priorities of US and European capital.

In practice, the adaptation fund is likely to act as a tool for taking control of important natural assets of poor countries. This applies particularly to these countries' forests—both the old-growth forests now being eyed as "carbon sinks", and new tree plantations.

Forest-related Carbon Offsets

The forests lie at the heart of a key financial "product" pioneered by the Kyoto system—"carbon offsets". Industrialists who pump carbon into the atmosphere can "offset" their transgressions by buying credits created by the planting of trees, which as they grow will absorb carbon dioxide. Or, emitters can buy credits created on the basis that governments and corporations graciously decide to leave existing forests intact.

Carbon offsets are a questionable proposition for a long list of reasons. How much carbon dioxide a forest will absorb over a given period is at best an educated guess. Forests can burn, releasing their carbon. Old-growth forests absorb much less carbon dioxide than new plantations, which enhances the temptation to clear-fell the former in order to plant the latter.

The forests lie at the heart of a key financial "product" pioneered by the Kyoto system—"carbon offsets".

The problems are multiplied wherever regulation is lax and officials corrupt. Tropical forests, it can be expected, will at times both be logged and claimed as carbon sinks. Where such forests are protected with any vigour, the "protection" is often likely to be aimed at indigenous people who practice a sustainable shifting agriculture. The increased incentives for plantation forestry threaten to cost tenant farmers their land.

So far, the most glaring absurdity to arise from the "carbon offset" provisions of the Kyoto Protocol has not appeared in the Third World, but in Australia. Though refusing to sign the Kyoto Protocol, the former Howard government regularly stressed that Australia was on track to meet its Kyoto targets.

Technically, this was true; on the basis of "offsets" earned through restrictions on additional land-clearing, Australia was permitted under Kyoto to increase its emissions by 8%.

The land-clearing, however, had already been encountering fierce criticism from environmentalists, and much of it would have been halted anyway. Meanwhile, fossil-fuel emissions from Australia's coal-fired economy have continued to boom. Supporters of carbon trading argue that potential critics should forgive the youthful fumbling of a previously untried system. But with the Bali Roadmap promising an extension and elaboration of carbon trading, the system's record in actually curbing greenhouse emissions deserves to be looked at.

There is no doubt that huge sums of money are changing hands—probably as much as US$60 billion in 2007. But even in the relatively orderly conditions of Europe, where the trading so far has been concentrated, the results in terms of greenhouse gas abatement have been lacklustre.

As of the end of 2005, emissions by the 15 "core" European Union countries were 2% below the Kyoto base year of 1990, compared to a target of 8% below by 2012. "Emissions have in fact been rising since the year 2000", a November 2005 Skyscrapper City report stated.

The December 5 *Australian* noted that the vast majority of Kyoto signatories were exceeding their emissions allowances, "in many cases by huge amounts". Most of them, the newspaper observed, have "given up on Kyoto", and are waiting for the Bali parameters to come into force after 2012.

Why Go with the Market?

If carbon trading has performed so badly, why persist with it? The question has been posed from some unlikely quarters. At the Bali conference, New York Republican Mayor Michael Bloomberg argued that the cap-and-trade system should be replaced by straight carbon taxes.

"It's a very inefficient way to accomplish the same thing that a carbon tax accomplishes", Bloomberg was quoted as saying of the cap-and-trade market. "It leaves itself open to special interests, corruption, inefficiencies."

Why, indeed, not simply make the polluters pay, using a combination of carbon taxes, state regulation and fines to force them to cut their emissions? Since the carbon trading system only covers relatively large emitters, keeping track of their emissions would be well within the capacities of a determined state apparatus, especially in developed countries.

The 1997 decision at Kyoto to go with carbon trading is especially curious since experience at the time pointed in the exact opposite direction. In the 1990s, various approaches had been tried in order to cut the sulphur dioxide pollution that was causing "acid rain". In the US, a cap-and-trade system had been instituted in 1990. By 2001, US levels of sulphur dioxide were down by 31%.

In Europe, a rule-based approach scored much better results. For Western Europe, the reduction was 57%.

As noted by Bloomberg, carbon trading "is attractive to many politicians because it doesn't have that three-letter word 'tax'". A key tenet of modern capitalist thought is the "need" to oust taxation, along with other forms of state intervention, from all possible areas of economic life.

But the real reason why carbon trading was selected at Kyoto goes deeper. It was summed up recently by British researcher Kevin Smith in a September 20 [2007] Transnational Institute article:

"The problem lies in the fact that carbon trading is designed with the express purpose of providing an opportunity for rich countries to delay making costly structural changes towards low-carbon technologies. This isn't a malfunction of the market or an unexpected byproduct: this is what the market was designed to do."

Once this real function of the carbon market is understood, a great deal else falls into place. The low price of emissions credits ceases to be a mystery. Key features of the carbon trading system—the over-allocation of free emissions permits in the EU [European Union], the far-fetched offset credits, and more—take on their true shape as devices for keeping the costs of polluting to a minimum.

That is not to say that a shift to rules and taxes would, of itself, cure the problems. In any battle between polluting corporations and aggrieved populations, capitalist governments stand, to the extent that mass pressures permit, with the polluters.

The problem, in short, is capitalism.

Carbon May Become the Largest Commodity Market in the World

James Kanter

James Kanter is a reporter who covers European and global business issues for the International Herald Tribune, *an English-language international newspaper.*

Seeking to match a desire to make money with his environmental instincts, Louis Redshaw, a former electricity trader, met with five top investment banks to propose trading carbon dioxide. Only one, Barclays Capital, was interested in his proposition.

Three years later, the situation has turned around entirely, and carbon experts like Redshaw, 34, are among the rising stars in the City of London financial district. Managing emissions is one of the fastest-growing segments in financial services, and companies are scrambling for talent. Their goal: a slice of a market now worth about $30 billion, but which could grow to $1 trillion within a decade.

[The carbon market] could grow to $1 trillion within a decade.

"Carbon will be the world's biggest commodity market, and it could become the world's biggest market overall," said Redshaw, the head of environmental markets at Barclays Capital. But he said that in his current job, unlike some of his previous ones, including a stint as a British power trader at Enron, "I don't have to compromise on anything when I get out of bed in the morning."

London at the Center

If greed is suddenly good for the environment, then the seed-bed for this vast new financial experiment is London. A report released [in June 2007] ... by International Financial Services London, a company promoting British-based financial services, said that British companies were the leading global investors in carbon projects and that more carbon was traded in London than in any other city.

The rapid emergence of carbon finance in London—not only trading carbon allowances but investments in projects that help to generate additional credits—is largely the result of a decision by European governments to start capping amounts that industries emit.

Factories and plants that pollute too much are required to buy more allowances; those that become more efficient can sell allowances they no longer need at a profit. The system, started in 2005, is part of the Kyoto Protocol [an international agreement to cut greenhouse gas emissions] and bears the imprimatur of the United Nations. Even so, doubts remain as to whether carbon finance can deliver tangible emissions reductions, let alone the huge economic transformation needed to tackle climate change.

For now, however, green-minded graduates and an eclectic range of professionals from banks, consulting companies and aid organizations are eagerly joining one of the most vibrant new sectors in London finance.

"We don't have to advertise," said Mark Woodall, 45, the chief executive of Climate Change Capital, an investment company based in an elegant 18th-century townhouse in the heart of the upscale Mayfair district of London. "People feel quite good about working in an organization like this."

Woodall has a staff of 120 employees with an average age of about 30 and more than 10 full-time employees in China. He is moving to larger offices to accommodate the additional 80 people he expects to hire over the next two years.

To be sure, carbon traders and investors do not yet make the same staggering amounts of money as some of their counterparts in foreign exchange and corporate finance.

European governments handed out too many free allowances in preparing for the start of the [carbon trading] program, rendering the system less effective than was hoped.

But remuneration is rising rapidly. A successful financier at Climate Change Capital, which manages a fund worth $1.25 billion to invest in credit-generating projects, might in a very good year take home as much as 10 times the basic salary, Woodall said.

"Do we pay the same as top investment banks? Not today, but maybe tomorrow," said Woodall, a former British Army officer who started his first company 15 years ago cleaning up waste and chemical spills.

Good Prospects

The industry has run into criticism. One reason is that European governments handed out too many free allowances in preparing for the start of the program, rendering the system less effective than was hoped. The over-allocation fueled volatility, and some traders reaped fatter-than-expected profits.

Controversy has also dogged some of the projects promoted by the financiers to generate new credits.

Prospects for the [carbon] industry are good, especially if the United States joins Europe in establishing a trading system.

But overall, prospects for the industry are good, especially if the United States joins Europe in establishing a trading system, said Imtiaz Ahmad, 34, senior carbon trader for Morgan

Stanley in London. Ahmad has already lured a senior European Union environment official and a BP [British Petroleum] employee to join his three-member trading team, and he plans to hire more.

Human activities create about 38 billion tons of carbon dioxide each year, and governments regulate only a fraction of that amount. But if more governments decide to cut billions more tons of emissions, as leaders of industrialized nations discussed this month [June 2007] in Germany, and if the existing system in Europe is enlarged to cover transportation, there will be many more credits available—and a lot more finance and trading.

Individuals Can Purchase Carbon Offsets in a Voluntary Market

Rebecca Gallagher

Rebecca Gallagher worked as a 2007 summer intern for Sustainable Lawrence, a large group of residents, businesses, congregations, and other organizations dedicated to creating a sustainable community in Lawrence Township, New Jersey.

Every day people do dozens of things that put more carbon dioxide into the atmosphere. This gas is the main perpetrator of climate change, yet activities like driving, heating your house, air travel, and electricity consumption, are hard to stop. Individuals that want to reduce their "carbon footprint", the amount of carbon dioxide generated in a year, have the option of buying carbon offsets, often called renewable energy credits, or RECs.

[Carbon offset] projects can include ... planting trees (carbon sequestration), erecting wind turbines or solar panels, ... or updating manufacturing processes.

Carbon offsets are projects that decrease the amount of greenhouse gases (GHG) like carbon dioxide in the air to counterbalance the amount that an individual has emitted. These projects can include, but aren't limited to planting trees (carbon sequestration), erecting wind turbines or solar panels, reducing methane (a greenhouse gas more potent, but less common than carbon dioxide), or updating manufacturing processes to use less fossil fuel.

Rebecca Gallagher, "Carbon Offsets Explained," *Sustainable Lawrence: Sustaining Earth & Life in Lawrence.* www.sustainablelawrence.org. Reproduced by permission.

Two Examples

To offset the average US household energy consumption of 10,656 kWh [kilowatt hour, a unit of energy] per year, 3Phases, a large wind company in the Midwest, charges $213.00. 3Phases will use this money to produce, in theory, 10,656 kWh *extra* in wind energy by building that many more turbines. This new renewable energy will be added to the grid in the place of conventional energy, like coal. The pricing of carbon offsets for alternative energy firms is based on the price difference between fossil fuel energy production and the alternative energy production per kilowatt hour. In all cases, the money from the offset purchase must instigate additional reductions by the company. Otherwise, the price of the credit will not accurately reflect the amount of GHG reductions it caused.

Community Energy Inc., a Pennsylvania-based organization operating in New Jersey, is one of several companies doing the same thing.

The Controversy

As offset purchases have become more popular, journalists and researchers have raised the alarm and cautioned consumers about offsets that do little more than make you feel good. The major concern centers on *additionality*. Carbon mitigation is only additional if it occurs at a level above the baseline level, also called "business as usual." Ideally, the offset you buy should initiate extra reductions that could not have happened without the money you spent. Additionality is hard to measure: large firms are already working to reduce their GHG-producing activities, and offset purchases, especially small ones, may not actually instigate enough new activity to fully offset the promised amount of kilowatt hours.

A recent *New York Times* article publicized these problems. "To many environmentalists, the carbon-neutral campaign is a sign of the times—easy on the sacrifice and big on the consumerism," Andrew Revkin reported in his piece *Carbon Neutral Is Hip, but Is It Green?* Revkin quotes Denis Hayes, a leading sustainability activist and expert; "the worst of the carbon-offset programs resemble the Catholic Church's sale of indulgences back before the Reformation," he says. "Instead of reducing their carbon footprints, people take private jets and stretch limos, and then think they can buy an indulgence to forgive their sins." In the past year, researchers discovered that Al Gore, director of the climate change documentary *An Inconvenient Truth*, has a carbon footprint twenty times the national average; his mansion consumes almost 221,000kWh (kilowatt hours) a year. Gore buys offsets to legitimize this enormous fossil fuel consumption, but many question if his offset purchase actually exempts him from his climate change "sin".

In the United States . . . the average person generates around 20 carbon tons per year.

Citizens in China use an average of 3 carbon tons per year, and in India, the average is less than half that. In the United States, however, the average person generates around 20 carbon tons per year. Many environmentalists feel we should be reducing our carbon consumption by taking big steps to change our personal and organizational habits and use different technologies and/or fuels, instead of taking the easier path of changing nothing, and spending money to transfer the reduction responsibility to others.

Different offset providers have different pricing schemes, which further complicates the issue of additionality. For example, the 10,656kWh for which 3Phases charged $213.00, NativeEnergy charges $96.00 to offset, and Carbonfund just $89.00. Naturally, consumers are drawn to the cheapest prices, yet these cheaper brands may have questionable additionality.

Currently, there are no standards or regulations on offset providers, putting responsibility on the consumer to find the most reliable offsets.

Buying Offsets

Most people familiar with the offset market, including offset providers, encourage individuals first to take steps to reduce the amount of energy they use before making an offset purchase. Conserving electrical energy by turning off lights and computers at night, buying fuel-efficient appliances and vehicles, and being an informed consumer about the food you buy can all make significant reductions in your carbon footprint. . . . After taking these steps, only carbon offsets can mitigate the remaining GHG emissions, allowing individuals to go completely "carbon neutral."

CHAPTER 2

Are Carbon Offsets Effective in Reducing Global Warming?

Chapter Preface

Although carbon trading seems to be one solution the world is moving toward in an effort to reduce global warming, another economic policy tool—a carbon tax—also has been discussed as a way to reduce global greenhouse gas emissions. In theory, both carbon trading and a carbon tax seek to achieve the same goal of establishing a market price for carbon emissions to motivate industries to consider environmental costs as part of doing business and to encourage them to cut back on the production of dangerous greenhouse gases in the atmosphere.

The carbon trading system, or cap-and-trade, works basically by capping the total amount of emissions and then allowing companies and countries a great deal of flexibility in trading carbon credits or offsets to reach the overall emissions reduction goal. Many people have praised this system as a market-based solution because it lets the market determine where emissions can be reduced most cheaply. A similar pollution trading scheme was used successfully in the United States in the 1980s to reduce air pollutants, and today carbon trading is supported by many large corporations as well as many leaders in the environmental movement.

Cap-and-trade, however, has several disadvantages. Critics claim that such a trading system, by allowing companies to simply buy carbon credits to offset their carbon pollution, discourages companies that contribute the most to global warming from taking actions to cut their carbon emissions directly. The price of carbon credits also can be volatile, depending on various factors such as the rate of a country's economic growth, and the setting of emissions targets in a carbon trading system might be subject to political maneuvering and corruption. Another criticism of cap-and-trade programs is that some carbon offset projects would have been implemented even without the award of a carbon credit—a concept known as "additionality"—meaning that such credits do precious little to reduce emissions. Still other criticisms focus on the difficulty of monitoring carbon reduction projects to make sure they are really being implemented and that they actually are contributing to the promised reduction in emissions.

For these and other reasons, some experts would prefer a carbon tax approach. A uniform tax on carbon production, in contrast to carbon trading, would tax the fossil fuels that produce emissions. This, supporters argue, would directly make environmental costs part of the market price of fuels, creating a truer and fairer price for carbon that would affect everyone equally. Such a system would allow industries to calculate their product costs more precisely and would provide a clear incentive for businesses to reduce carbon emissions. In turn, companies' desire to minimize emissions would likely spur private and public investment in alternative fuels and low-carbon technologies. In both developed and developing countries, a carbon tax also could provide governments with new revenues that could be invested in needed social programs, education, or business development.

As with carbon offsets, however, the idea of a carbon tax has its problems. Perhaps the biggest hurdle is that taxes of any kind are hard to sell politically in most countries, including the United States. It also might be difficult to estimate exactly how large the carbon tax should be to achieve the intended benefits of emissions reductions. And getting governments around the world to standardize their carbon taxes could be much more difficult than setting up a global carbon trading market. Nevertheless, a few countries—such as Norway, Sweden, Finland, and Denmark—have enacted carbon taxes already, and these tax schemes have reportedly helped to reduce emissions slightly since the 1990s. The taxes also have raised significant new revenues and, in some cases, have helped to initiate research and development of green technologies, all without damaging national economies.

Although the Kyoto Protocol and most countries now favor carbon trading over carbon taxes, the two approaches may not be mutually exclusive. Former U.S. Vice President Al Gore, for example, has suggested taxing certain corporations that are heavy greenhouse gas polluters in addition to allowing them to participate in carbon trading. Carbon trading, therefore, potentially could be combined with some types of carbon taxes in a hybrid system in the future. For example, a company that expects to exceed government-imposed caps on emissions could be given the choice to either buy carbon credits or to pay an emissions tax. This hybrid option could become more attractive as more questions are raised about the effectiveness of the current carbon trading mechanisms adopted as part of the Kyoto treaty. Whether current carbon trading programs are, indeed, effective or ineffective in cutting carbon emissions is the subject of the viewpoints in this chapter.

Carbon Offsets Are One of Many Solutions Needed for Global Warming

David Suzuki

David Suzuki, co-founder of the David Suzuki Foundation, is an award-winning scientist, environmentalist, and broadcaster.

You may have been hearing a lot about carbon offsets, or 'carbon credits', lately. They've become a must-have accessory for individuals and organizations who want to fight climate change and show their green credentials.

Everyone from banks like HSBC [a New York-based corporate bank], to rock bands like the Rolling Stones, to almost 500 NHL [National Hockey League] players are purchasing carbon offsets for their emissions.

Carbon offsets are just one of the tools available to help us compensate for our emissions by making reductions somewhere else.

The Concept of Carbon Offsets

But what are carbon offsets anyway? And do they really help solve the problem of global warming?

As you know, greenhouse gas emissions—primarily from the burning of fuels such as coal, oil and gas—create heat-trapping gases in the atmosphere. (I like to think of the atmosphere as Earth's electric blanket.) These extra gases cause the thermostat of our "electric blanket" to go haywire, a phenomenon known as global warming.

If we are to have any hope of avoiding the most dire effects of global warming, humanity must reduce our collective

David Suzuki, "Science Matters: The Truth About Carbon Offsets," David Suzuki Foundation, February 22, 2008. Reproduced by permission. www.davidsuzuki.org.

greenhouse gas emissions. To do this, we must use energy more efficiently, and switch to renewable energy sources such as wind or solar power.

This transition will take some time and effort from the world's political leaders, companies, and citizens. But each one of us can make a difference by taking steps to reduce our greenhouse gas emissions.

As we make the transition to lower emissions, some of us have unavoidable activities that create greenhouse gases, like flying. Carbon offsets are just one of the tools available to help us compensate for our emissions by making reductions somewhere else.

It's important to choose offsets carefully, especially since the carbon offset market is new and mostly unregulated.

The concept is pretty simple. A carbon offset is a credit for a reduction in greenhouse gas emissions generated by one project, such as a wind farm, that can be used to balance the emissions from another source, such as a plane trip. Because greenhouse gases know no boundaries, it doesn't really matter where the reduction takes place.

For example, I still have to travel by air, which creates a lot of greenhouse gas emissions. (I'm working hard to reduce these emissions by cutting down on my flights, taking trains and buses and giving talks by video conferencing, which I can do from my office.) But for the flights I can't avoid, I calculate the emissions using an online calculator, and then purchase carbon offsets.

Buying Carbon Offsets

Which offsets do I buy? Well, it's important to choose offsets carefully, especially since the carbon offset market is new and mostly unregulated. If you're buying offsets, you should look for marks of quality, like the Gold Standard. Offsets that carry the Gold Standard label are regarded as the highest quality offsets in the world, and help fund new renewable energy projects. They are independently audited to ensure your purchase has a climate benefit. I purchase Gold Standard offsets for all of my flights, and my Foundation uses them too.

But as with anything new, there's been some misunderstanding around carbon offsets. For example, they've been criticized as "papal indulgences", or "buying your way out".

Carbon offsets are not a silver bullet, but global warming is such a big problem that it requires a whole range of solutions.

I see it differently. First of all, carbon offset are not an excuse for not reducing our emissions, but using high quality offsets—like those that meet the Gold Standard—can be an innovative way to deal with emissions that you aren't able to reduce yourself. Purchasing offsets can also have an important educational benefit. I've heard from people who've told me they decided to vacation closer to home after calculating their emissions to buy offsets for a trip abroad, and getting a true sense of the climate impact of flying.

In the fight against global warming, the use of market-based tools—like carbon offsets—is here to stay. For example, they are included in the Kyoto Protocol. And for good reason. The world's leading economists, including Sir Nicholas Stern, say that for us to reduce the use of fossil fuels, we must place a price on carbon to take into account the negative climate impact it has. Carbon offsets are a step in that direction. By voluntarily purchasing offsets for your emissions, you are recognizing the true cost of using fossil fuels, and helping to make clean energy sources more competitive.

Carbon offsets are not a silver bullet, but global warming is such a big problem that it requires a whole range of solutions. Carbon offsets are just one of them.

Carbon Trading Markets Are Working

Neal Dikeman

Neal Dikeman is a founding partner at Jane Capital Partners LLC, a boutique merchant bank advising strategic investors and startups in cleantech. He also is founding contributor of Cleantech Blog, a Web site featuring commentary on technologies, news, and issues related to next generation energy and the environment.

The carbon markets are an area of keen interest for me personally and professionally, so it is always frustrating that the mainstream media largely refuses to learn the details.

> The carbon markets ARE working, and are pouring billions of dollars into fighting global warming.

In general, layman and media who don't understand the details of the carbon markets attack carbon offsets in two areas, first, questioning whether the credits are for a project that would have occurred anyway (a concept known in carbon as "additionality"), and second questioning whether there are checks and balances to ensure the environmental standards are adhered to and the abatement actually happens (in carbon known as the validation and verification processes). The frustrating part for anyone in the industry is that the entire carbon credit process set up under Kyoto [an international agreement to cut greenhouse gas emissions] is all about ensuring the answers to those two questions. Leading certification firms and carbon project developers have been dealing with the details behind those questions for years.

Neal Dikeman, "Carbon Offsets Work—Will the Mainstream Media Ever Get It?" *Cleantech Blog,* May 19, 2008. Reproduced by permission of the author. www.cleantechblog .com.

The biggest weakness of the carbon offset process to date has been that the high level of oversight and protection, while working, has led to higher costs and fewer projects getting done, rather than too many. Bottom line, the carbon markets ARE working, and are pouring billions of dollars into fighting global warming, just like the NOx [nitrogen oxide] and SOx [sulfur oxide] trading markets helped reduce air pollution faster and cheaper than anyone expected. Now it's time to figure out how to make them *really* scale.

I caught up with a friend of mine, Marc Stuart, to give us a little teach in about the real story in carbon offsets, what matters, what does not, what works, and what still needs to be tweaked. Marc should know, he's one of the founders of Eco-Securities plc, one of the first, and still the leader in generating and monetizing carbon credits. Marc, thanks for joining us, we appreciate the time and the teach in.

Additionality . . . means that a developer cannot receive [carbon] credits for a project that represents "business as usual" (BAU) practices.

The Concept of Additionality

Neal Dikeman: Even for those who don't know much about carbon offsets, many people have heard about the concept of additionality, and almost everyone intuitively understands it at some level. But it is devilishly complicated in practice. I've always described it to people as "beyond business as usual". Can you explain additionality and give us some insight into the details?

Marc Stuart: Additionality is the core concept of the project-based emissions market. In a nutshell, it means that a developer cannot receive credits for a project that represents "business as usual" (BAU) practices. A classic and often cited example is that industrial forest companies should not be able to get credits simply for replanting the trees that they harvest from their plantations each year, since that is already part of their business model. A utility changing out a 30 year old, fully depreciated turbine would not be able to claim the efficiency benefits, though a utility that swapped out something only five years old might be able to under certain circumstances.

Additionality is easy to definitively prove in cases where there is zero normal economic reason to make an investment, such as reducing HFC-23 [trifluoromethane] from the refrigeration plants or N_2O [nitrous oxide] from fertilizer plants. Such projects easily pass a "financial additionality" test, since it's clear that as a cost without a benefit, they wouldn't have been economically feasible under a BAU scenario. It gets far more complex though, with assets that contribute to both normal economic outputs and the development of carbon credits, in particular in renewables and energy efficiency. Sometimes these projects are profitable without carbon finance, but there may be other barriers preventing their execution that make them additional.

Like it or not, GHG emissions from the industrial world are going to take quite a while to stabilize and reduce.

The UN [United Nations] has developed a very structured and rigorous process that projects must undergo to prove additionality. It is essentially a regulatory process with multiple levels of oversight, in which a body called the Executive Board to the UN's Clean Development Mechanism (The CDM is the international system for creating carbon offsets called CERs) ultimately makes a binding decision about whether a project is eligible to participate or not. Anchored in the middle of that oversight is an audit process run by independent, licensed auditors, the largest of which is actually a multi-national nonprofit called Det Norske Veritas (DNV). However, many projects don't even make it to that decision point before they are dropped in the process.

One of the benefits of carbon offsets often touted by those who support them is the idea that they provide compliance flexibility and liquidity in the early years of a compliance cap-and-trade system. What are your thoughts on how that works?

The simple reality is that many assets that emit carbon have long lifetimes and that legitimate investment decisions have been taken in the past that rightfully did not take into account the negative impact of carbon emissions. For an easy example, think about somebody who is a couple of years into a six-year auto loan on a gas guzzler—can policy just force that person to immediately switch to a hybrid, especially since the used car market for his guzzler has now completely disappeared? Even if society says yes, how long would it take for the auto industry to ramp up its production of hybrids? Now look at infrastructure—for example, most power plants and heavy industry facilities have lifetimes of thirty years plus. Even if we were economically and politically able to affect a radical changeover, simply put, the physical capacity for building out new technology is limited, even in a highly accelerated scenario. So, like it or not, GHG [greenhouse gas] emissions from the industrial world are going to take quite a while to stabilize and reduce.

The point of offsets is that, in fairly carbon efficient places like California or Japan, availability of low cost reductions within a cap-and-trade system is quite limited, meaning there is an incentive to look beyond the cap for other, credible, quantifiable, emissions reductions. Reductions in GHGs that are uncapped (either by sector, activity, or geography), such as are found in the CDM, are thus a logical way to achieve real GHG reductions and accelerate dissemination of low carbon technologies. In effect, the past helps subsidize changeover to the future as buyers of emission rights subsidize other, cheaper,

GHG mitigation activities. As caps get more restrictive over time, capital changeover occurs. Offsets allow this to occur in an orderly and cost-effective manner.

There have been a number of studies questioning whether offsets are just "hot air" and whether carbon offset projects actually achieve real emission reductions. What is your response to these accusations?

Determining an individual emission baseline for a [carbon offset] project—the metric against which emission reductions are measured—is a challenging process.

As noted in the first question, the CDM in particular is a market that is completely regulated by an international body of experts supported by extensive bureaucracy to ensure that real emission reductions and sustainable development are occurring. The first and foremost requirement of that body is to rule on whether each individual project is additional. Each project is reviewed by qualified Operational Entity, the Executive Board Registration and Issuance Team, the UNFCCC [United Nations Framework Convention on Climate Change, an international treaty on climate change] CDM Secretariat and the CDM Executive Board itself. Plus, there are multiple occasions for external observers to make specific comments, which are given significant weight. So, while there is always the chance something could get through, there are a lot of checks and balances in the system to prevent that.

That said, determining an individual emission baseline for a project—the metric against which emission reductions are measured—is a challenging process. The system adjusts to those challenges by trying to be as conservative as possible. In other words, I would argue that in most CDM projects, there are fewer emission reductions being credited than are actually occurring. It is impossible for a hypothetical baseline to be absolutely exact, but it is eminently possible to be conservative. Is it inconceivable that the opposite occasionally occurs and that more emission reductions are credited to a project than are real? We've never seen it in the more than 117 projects we've registered with the CDM, but I suppose it's possible.

The voluntary market has had more of a "wild west" reputation compared to the compliance market.

The Voluntary Carbon Market

What about the voluntary carbon market in the US, where there have been accusations that many projects would have happened anyway? How is this voluntary market different from what Eco-Securities does under the Clean Development Mechanism?

The voluntary market has had more of a "wild west" reputation compared to the compliance market. In some ways, that is deserved, but in some ways it is unfair. For a number of years, the voluntary market was the only outlet for project developers in places like the United States and in sectors like avoided deforestation that were not recognized by the CDM. However, because there were virtually no barriers to entry and no functional regulation other than what providers would voluntarily undertake, it was difficult for consumers and companies to differentiate between legitimate providers and charlatans. For EcoSecurities, while the voluntary market has been a very small part of our overall efforts, we always qualified projects according to vetted additionality standards such as the CDM and the California Climate Action Registry, and always used independent accredited auditors. With the emergence of stand-alone systems like the Voluntary Carbon Standard, and the growing demand for offsets from the corporate sector, I believe the "wild west" frontier is drawing to a close.

It is also important to note that while the voluntary market has recorded very explosive growth, it is still a very small fraction of the regulatory market, comprising a few tens of millions of dollars of transactions, versus the potential tens of billions of dollars of value embedded in the highly regulated and supervised CDM. The fact that many observers still equate the occasional problems in the fringes of the voluntary market with the real benefits being created in the Kyoto compliance market is a misperception we'd like to correct.

While the voluntary [carbon offset] market has recorded very explosive growth, it is still a very small fraction of the regulatory market.

What about these projects we've heard about in China, where the sale of carbon credits generated from HFC-23 capture is far more valuable than production of the refrigerant gas that leads to its creation in the first place? How is this being addressed in the CDM and how can future systems ensure that there are not perverse incentives created like this?

HFC-23 projects are the epitome of what is often referred to as "low hanging fruit." In this case, most of the fruit might have actually been sitting on the ground. While there is no doubt in anybody's mind that the market drove the mitigation of HFC-23 globally, the extreme disparity between the costs of reducing those gases and the market value those reductions commanded invariably led to questions whether there were more socially efficient ways to have reduced those emissions. In all likelihood, there were. But to catalyze an overall market like this, it is probably important to get some easy wins at the outset to create broader investment interest and this certainly accomplished that. Moreover, Kyoto created a mechanism for engaging these kinds of activities. It would have sent a much worse signal to the market to have changed the rules in the middle of the game. The CDM has subsequently adjusted the rules to make sure that no one can put new factories in place simply for the purposes of mitigating their emissions. I don't see too many other situations like HFCs in the future, simply because there are no other gases where the disparity of mitigation costs and market value is so severe.

Binding Targets

Given that the majority of CDM projects currently under development are located in China and India, how can we ensure that these countries eventually take on the binding targets we will need to reach the scientifically determined reductions in GHGs? Doesn't the CDM simply create an incentive for these countries to avoid binding targets as long as possible?

It is clearly in the world's interest to get as much of the global economy into a low carbon trajectory as quickly as possible. However, it is politically unrealistic to expect these countries—whose emissions per capita are between one fifth and one tenth the per capita of the United States—to make an equivalent commitment at this juncture, particularly considering that they are in the midst of an aggressive development trajectory. The CDM provides a way for ongoing engagement with these countries, developing the basic architecture of a lower carbon economy. And there is no doubt that China's emissions in 2012, 2015 or 2020 will be measurably lower than they otherwise would have been, simply because of the current accomplishments of the CDM. Over time, the use of project based mechanisms will contribute to accelerating the development and dissemination of low carbon technologies, which will make those negotiations for binding caps from all major economies far more tenable.

Analysis . . . of the ETS [European Union Emissions Trading System] shows that there were real emission reductions undertaken within the system.

It is widely believed that to address the climate crisis on the scale necessary to avert dangerous global warming, significant infrastructural and paradigm shifts must occur at an unprec-

edented scale. Some people are concerned that offsets provide a disincentive for making these shifts, since companies can just offset their emissions instead of making the changes themselves. Is this something you saw under the EU ETS [European Union Emissions Trading System] at all, and if so, how can it be addressed in a US system?

Virtually all of the macroeconomic analysis that has been done of Phase I of the ETS shows that there were real emission reductions undertaken within the system, despite the fact that many companies were also actively seeking CDM CERs. Clearly the fact that both Kyoto and the EU ETS system place quantifiable limits on the use of CDM and Joint Implementation (JI) [another type of carbon offset program created by the Kyoto treaty] credits guarantees that emission reductions will also be made in-country as well, so pure "outsourcing" of emissions compliance is not possible. This also appears to be the model being pursued in most US legislation.

The project by project approval approach is creating logistical challenges as the [carbon offset] system [grows].

Many have complained that the CDM system is too administratively complex, unpredictable, and that the transaction costs of the system are so significant that they could almost negate any possible benefits. What lessons can be learned about structuring an offset system in a simpler, but still environmentally rigorous way? What steps is the CDM EB [Clean Development Mechanism Executive Board] taking to address these issues?

The CDM treads a very fine line between ensuring environmental integrity of the offsets that it certifies and the need to have some kind of efficient process within an enormous global regulatory enterprise. To date, one has to think that they have gotten it about right, as business has complained about inefficiency and environmentalists have complained about environmental integrity. However, it is becoming increasingly clear that the project by project approval approach is creating logistical challenges as the system graduates from managing dozens, to hundreds, to now, quite literally, thousands of projects in all corners of the world. Ironically, it is the success of the CDM in terms of its very broad uptake by carbon entrepreneurs that is causing problems for the current model.

We believe the benefits of the CDM can be maintained by moving many project types into a more standardized approach, whereby emission reduction coefficients are determined "top-down" by a regulatory body, as opposed to being undertaken individually for every project by project proponents. For example, there are dozens of highly similar wind energy projects in China that all have microscopically different emission baselines. A conservative top down baseline set by the regulator would enable projects to get qualified by the system in an efficient manner with far less bureaucratic overhang. This is how California's Climate Action Reserve deals with project based reductions and we think that it could work well for many sectors.

Carbon Offsets Help to Mitigate the Environmental Harm from Air Travel

Joelle Novey

Joelle Novey is an editorial assistant for Co-op America, a national nonprofit helping people use their economic power for a more socially just and environmentally sustainable society.

A decade ago, a group of European scientists set out for the UN [United Nations] Climate Convention in Kyoto, Japan—without getting on a plane. Determined not to "contribute . . . to the problem that the convention was intended to solve," they traveled across Europe and then through Siberia and China to Japan by train, boat and bike over the course of several weeks.

Even for those of use who aren't ready to completely swear off traveling by air, the story of the "Climate Train" holds an important lesson about the climate impact of flying: A single international flight can emit as much greenhouse gas per passenger as a *year* of driving.

At those times when we have no choice but to take a journey by plane, we can still mitigate the harm to the environment caused by the flight by offsetting the emissions from that trip.

Carbon Offsets Defined

By purchasing carbon offsets, you help fund a project that prevents one ton of greenhouse gases from being emitted for each ton that you have caused. Carbon offset providers sell the greenhouse gas reductions associated with projects like wind farms or methane-capture facilities to customers who want to offset the emissions they caused by flying, driving, or using electricity. (Though they're called "carbon" offsets, they offset all greenhouse gases that cause global warming, from carbon dioxide to methane.)

[If] we have no choice but to take a journey by plane, we can still mitigate the harm to the environment caused by the flight by offsetting the emissions from that trip.

For example, if a scientist had had no choice but to fly to the Kyoto convention, she couldn't prevent that flight from producing tons of greenhouse gases (GHGs). But she could balance out that impact by investing in a project that reduces global warming emissions, such as a new wind power project that displaces coal energy.

By purchasing carbon offsets, you help fund a project that prevents one ton of greenhouse gases from being emitted for each ton that you have caused.

That's where carbon offset programs come in. They help a traveler easily calculate how much of an investment will result in a GHG reduction to match the GHGs generated by her share of the flight. By making that investment and offsetting her flight, a traveler can make her plane trip essentially "carbon neutral."

Carbon offsetting is one of many economic actions you can take to address climate change, and it is a powerful one. Many promising projects that would help to reduce greenhouse gas emissions lack the capital they need to get built; by directing your offset dollars to these projects, you can help finance new wind farms, solar arrays, and more.

First Step: Do the Math

The first step to reducing the net climate impact of your travel is to calculate how many tons of GHGs will be emitted over the course of your trip. Use an online calculator such as the one offered by *Native*Energy [an offset provider]. A round trip flight from Washington, DC, to San Francisco, for example, emits more than two tons of GHGs per passenger.

A Variety of Options

Once you know how many tons of GHGs you've added to the atmosphere, select an offset that will reduce GHGs by the same amount. While it's no replacement for reducing our carbon emissions to begin with, buying carbon offsets is a "compelling way to channel funds to projects that will result in a low-carbon future," says Adam Stein of TerraPass [an offset provider].

Your offset purchases can support a wide variety of forward-thinking projects that reduce GHG emissions, including:

- *Green tags from current renewable energy generation.*
  Energy customers who wish to support wind and solar power can already do so by purchasing renewable energy certificates, also known as "RECs," or "green tags." Green tags represent the environmental benefits generated by existing green energy facilities like wind turbines or solar arrays. Consumers without green power options can purchase green tags as a way of supporting renewable energy generation. Or, utility companies that offer their customers green energy options may simply purchase green tags on their behalf from an outside green power facility, rather than building their own.

  Because putting more renewable energy into the electric grid will, over time, reduce the energy that GHG-spewing coal plants need to put in, renewable energy also promises to reduce global warming emissions. Therefore, some carbon offset providers sell green tags as carbon offsets. For example, the Climate Trust [an offset provider] offers green tag offsets associated with wind farms in Oregon.

- *Green tags from future renewable energy projects. Native*Energy takes an innovative approach to selling green tags as offsets. Instead of offering them from existing green energy facilities, it sells green tags from facilities that are yet to be built, representing the environmental benefits these future projects will generate. In this way, green tag and offset purchases through *Native*Energy help fund construction of new wind turbines and other projects. Better still, these green energy projects are all owned and operated by Native American tribes and small-scale farmers in the US, providing economic benefits to these populations.

  In short, *Native*Energy's model makes new green energy facilities financially viable that would have otherwise lacked the capital to go forward, increasing clean energy generation capacity and building the infrastructure for a low-carbon future.

- *Sustainable development projects.* Some providers use offset purchases to fund "clean development" projects in developing countries, which both fight poverty and reduce GHG emissions. *MyClimate* [an offset provider] has created a small hydraulic power station in Indonesia that will generate clean, reliable energy for a Sumatran community. In Eritrea, they have installed hundreds of solar water heaters for schools.

- *Farm and landfill methane projects. Native*Energy also uses offset purchases to install methane digesters on family farms in Pennsylvania to capture methane, a potent greenhouse gas generated by livestock. "Digesters" use the methane to generate power. Other offset providers support similar projects to capture and convert methane that rises out of landfills.

- *Other projects.* Offset providers support other creative projects that reduce GHG emissions. *The Climate Trust* sells offsets to fund the electrification of truck stops, so trucks won't have to idle while they're waiting to refuel, and to support a "Climate Cool Concrete" program that gets Portland construction projects to use a blended cement that causes lower emissions.

The market in carbon offsets has grown rapidly, and standards for the industry are still evolving.

What to Look For

The market in carbon offsets has grown rapidly, and standards for the industry are still evolving. Particularly because you can't see or touch a reduction of greenhouse gases, and because prices per ton vary widely among providers, purchasing a reputable offset can be confusing.

"Almost anyone can offer to sell you almost anything and claim that this purchase will make you carbon-neutral," concludes a recent study by Trexler Climate + Energy Services. "It is very difficult for consumers . . . to differentiate between a high-quality and a low-quality offering."

For an offset purchase to be meaningful, the purchase [should not take] . . . credit for a reduction that would have happened anyway.

Below, we offer a few general guidelines for selecting a high-quality carbon offset:

- *Reduce your impact first.* Only purchase a carbon offset after you've looked for ways to reduce your emissions by flying less, driving less, driving a higher mileage car, or reducing your home energy use.

- *Look for offsets that supports specific projects.* Don't settle for a vague claim from an offset provider. When travelers purchase a Flight TerraPass, for example, they receive a "product content label" describing the specific carbon-reducing projects "contained" in their offset.

- *Look for offsets that will cause carbon reductions that wouldn't have happened otherwise.* For an offset purchase to be meaningful, the purchase has to cause a new carbon reduction corresponding with the new emissions you caused, rather than taking credit for a reduction that would have happened anyway. MyClimate, for example, is careful to support specific clean development projects where their investment will make the difference between the project happening (and reducing GHGs) or not happening.

- *Look for offsets whose GHG reductions will happen on a clear timeframe.* Ask offset providers when the offset you are buying today will result in a reduction, and use that information in selecting a provider.

- *Look for offset providers that ensure your offset can't be re-sold.* Offset providers deal in an invisible product, so they must take pains to demonstrate that they sell each offset only once. For example, *Native*Energy retires all green tags purchased as offsets by donating them to a nonprofit so they can't be double-sold.

- *Look for offset providers that are independently verified.* There is currently no common standard or certification that guarantees offset quality. The best offset providers find various ways to assure customers that a knowledgeable third party has examined and approved their practices. For example, TerraPass hired the Center for Resource Solutions (CRS) to perform an independent audit of their program, and it made the document available online.

Several organizations, including CRS and the Climate Group (TCG), are currently working with offset providers to develop a common standard for carbon offsets. A certification of offsets, such as CRS' "green-e Greenhouse Gas Reduction Standard," or TCG's "Voluntary Carbon Standard," may be available to guide customers within the coming year. We'll announce it in our *Real Money* newsletter when new shared standards and certifications become available.

- *Avoid offsets based on tree-planting projects.* Planting trees feels good, and projects that plant trees can be easier to love than projects involving something as mundane as cow methane or cement. However, there are much better offset programs than those that involve trees. It's very hard to calculate how much CO_2 a given forest will "breathe in." And, some offset providers base their calculations for a tree planted today on the CO_2 it will take in over its entire lifetime, which is decades after the emissions associated with the flight or drive being offset. Bottom line: when it comes to carbon offsets, planting trees is not the best bet. However, planting trees has other environmental benefits, and we encourage tree planting for these reasons.

- *Avoid offsets that purchase "allowances" on a climate exchange.* When companies want to reduce their emissions, they can trade GHG reductions that exceeded their targets with other companies by using the Chicago Climate Exchange (CCX). CCX does good work in

the business sector, but you may want to avoid purchasing offsets based on CCX allowances.

Offset providers that purchase allowances from the
CCX and offer them to individuals as carbon offsets
often cannot name the specific projects that generated
the reductions they are selling. Offset customers have a
right to know exactly what reduction they are purchasing, and to receive assurances that it wouldn't have
happened without their purchase.

If you're a conscientious consumer who tries to live a
low-emission lifestyle, consider offsetting the remaining
emissions for which you are responsible. And spread
the word to others—many offset vendors will send a
luggage tag when you purchase air travel offsets or a
bumper sticker when you purchase car offsets.

Carbon Offsets Are Better Than Doing Nothing About Carbon Emissions

The Carbon Consultancy

The Carbon Consultancy is an organization located in the United Kingdom that provides carbon measurement and reduction strategies primarily for the travel sector.

Carbon offsets are worthwhile if used as part of an integrated carbon management programme that includes emissions reduction as a primary aim. They are better than doing nothing about emissions, but not a substitute for emissions reduction. Best practice in carbon management dictates that they are to be used for those emissions that cannot be saved. The purpose of an offset is to balance a quantity of emissions with a corresponding saving, through carbon storage or carbon saving projects. The offset alone will not prevent carbon induced climate change, but they are an important part of the drive to stabilise atmospheric carbon at 550 parts per million by 2050. In the crudest sense they are helping to buy time whilst behavioural change, technology and legislation begin to actually reduce emissions.

A Licence to Pollute?

Media scrutiny of offsets frequently portrays them as a licence to pollute, sold by companies motivated solely by profit and deliver highly questionable project benefits. This emotive portrayal rarely examines their value and the context in which they should be assessed. It has had the effect of confusing individuals and companies alike and created a paralysis of action through a failure to explore the role and relevance of offset.

"What Is the Value and Role of Carbon Offset?" The Carbon Consultancy, 2007. Reproduced by permission. www.thecarbonconsultancy.co.uk.

There is no such thing as a licence to pollute, and responsible offset providers are full service carbon management companies helping corporate and individual customers to reduce emissions. There may indeed be the carbon equivalent of the collapse of Barings [a British bank], which even the forthcoming government standards may not prevent, just as the heavy regulation of the financial sector failed to save Barings. However, any balanced examination of the voluntary and certified offset sector will find valuable carbon benefits being delivered by committed practitioners.

Media scrutiny of [carbon] offsets frequently portrays them as a license to pollute.

The offset is frequently used as a primary engagement tool, with purchasers gaining their first experience of carbon calculation and action. This process involves calculation and initially delivers an understanding of how activity links to carbon at a micro level, in an environment dominated by macro level information. Responsible offset providers promote reduction alongside mitigation and this educational function is key to developing the awareness and behavioural change that is so essential to emissions reduction.

Offset purchase as an alternative to reduction is not a realistic or sustainable stance to adopt and is not a suggestion that will be found from the carbon management community. This has not prevented a number of high profile companies declaring "Carbon Neutral" status based primarily upon offset purchase, but the consequence of this may be a consumer backlash as consumers become more carbon literate. The claim of carbon neutrality implies a state of grace that is illusory and adds to the notion that carbon emissions reduction is easy to achieve, which it is not.

How Offsets Work

At a government level the international community have decided upon emissions cap and trade as a mechanic to limit and reduce emissions. The offset unit forms part of this cap and trade approach and is crudely designed to tax polluters and turn their money into carbon storage and reduction. Voluntary offsets are a voluntary tax and subject to credible projects, perform the same function. This is an infinitely superior mechanic to the government taking another £1 billion [one billion British pounds, or roughly 1.7 billion U.S. dollars] in Air Passenger Duty increases as a green tax, which does nothing to reduce emissions.

There is however no substitute for reducing our emissions as an urgent and primary carbon policy.

For offsets to be effective they must be matched by proper calculations. All emissions from travel relate directly to the carbon content of the fuel used. This is calculated for company emissions auditing purposes as an average. This average can be improved upon and is by some companies to help influence choice and policy. The frequent surprise demonstrated by many commentators in relation to carbon calculator discrepancies is always accompanied by a failure to examine the rationale behind underlying calculations and a demand for more standards. Most UK calculators use government reporting standards, some use their own research and some include a radiative forcing uplift. Those using their own research all indicate the methodology, allowing users to make up their own minds on their efficacy and suitability. There is no question now or in the next few years of calculation methods being available that are accurate to the last gram of carbon dioxide. Standards already exist and will improve. The clamour for more standards and the delivery of the last gram reporting is an easy excuse for inaction, in an environment where time is a commodity we are short of in the climate change challenge.

Offsets have a carbon value, but it must be placed in the context of our need to reduce emissions as a primary response. The secondary or even tertiary role of offsets in any carbon reduction programme does not diminish their value. More common sense and greater carbon literacy will allow consumers and companies to evaluate their role. The UK has no ring fenced green taxes, creating a climate where emitters are obliged to use non governmental routes to achieve tangible carbon emissions mitigation. There is however no substitute for reducing our emissions as an urgent and primary carbon policy.

A Majority of the United Nations' Carbon Offset Projects Do Nothing To Cut Global Warming

John Vidal

John Vidal is the environment editor for The Guardian, *a well-known newspaper in the United Kingdom.*

Billions of pounds are being wasted in paying industries in developing countries to reduce climate change emissions, according to two analyses of the UN's [United Nations] carbon offsetting programme.

Leading academics and watchdog groups allege that the UN's main offset fund is being routinely abused by chemical, wind, gas and hydro companies who are claiming emission reduction credits for projects that should not qualify. The result is that no genuine pollution cuts are being made, undermining assurances by the UK [United Kingdom] government and others that carbon markets are dramatically reducing greenhouse gases, the researchers say.

Criticisms of the CDM System

The criticism centres on the UN's clean development mechanism (CDM), an international system established by the Kyoto process that allows rich countries to meet emissions targets by funding clean energy projects in developing nations.

Credits from the project are being bought by European companies and governments who are unable to meet their carbon reduction targets.

The market for CDM credits is growing fast. At present it is worth nearly $20bn a year, but this is expected to grow to over $100bn within four years. More than 1,000 projects have so far been approved, and 2,000 more are making their way through the process.

A working paper from two senior Stanford University academics examined more than 3,000 projects applying for or already granted up to $10bn of credits from the UN's CDM funds over the next four years, and concluded that the majority should not be considered for assistance. "They would be built anyway," says David Victor, law professor at the Californian university. "It looks like between one and two thirds of all the total CDM offsets do not represent actual emission cuts."

Governments consider that CDM is vital to reducing global emissions under the terms of the Kyoto treaty. To earn credits under the mechanism, emission reductions must be in addition to those that would have taken place without the project. But critics argue this "additionality" is impossible to prove and open to abuse. The Stanford paper, by Victor and his colleague Michael Wara, found that nearly every new hydro, wind and natural gas-fired plant expected to be built in China in the next four years is applying for CDM credits, even though it is Chinese policy to encourage these industries.

A separate study . . . argues that nearly three quarters of all registered CDM projects were complete at the time of approval.

"Traders are finding ways of gaining credits that they would never have had before. You will never know accurately, but rich countries are clearly overpaying by a massive amount," said Victor.

A separate study published this week by US watchdog group International Rivers argues that nearly three quarters of all registered CDM projects were complete at the time of approval, suggesting that CDM money was not needed to finance them.

"It would seem clear that a project that is already built cannot need extra income in order to be built," said Patrick McCully, director of the thinktank in California. "Judging additionality has turned out to be unknowable and unworkable. It can never be proved definitively that if a developer or factory owner did not get offset income they would not build their project."

Yesterday a spokesman for the CDM in Bonn said the fund was significantly cutting emissions and providing incentives for companies to employ clean technologies: "There is a responsible level of scrutiny. The process is in continual reform. All the projects are vetted independently and are then certified by third parties. There are many checks and balances and we can show how all projects are vetted."

The UK government last night defended the CDM. "We completely reject any assertions that [it] is fundamentally flawed," a spokeswoman said. "We've worked consistently for and seen improvement in CDM processes over the past few years of its operation. We believe the CDM is essentially transparent and robust, though we will continue to press for the environmental integrity of projects."

The Only Beneficiaries of Carbon Offsets Are Polluting Corporations

Kevin Smith

Kevin Smith is a London-based researcher with Carbon Trade Watch, which is a project of the Transnational Institute, an international network of activist-scholars committed to critical analyses of global problems.

If, as their proponents claim, carbon markets are wonderful tools for bringing about emissions reductions and provide economic support for clean technologies in the global south [a reference to the developing world], then we should ask one question: why have they been met with a mounting chorus of criticism from civil-society organisations, social movements and journalists around the world?

Plans are being made, through processes like the G8+5 Climate Dialogue [a group composed of Canada, France, Germany, Italy, Japan, Russia, the United Kingdom, the United States, China, Brazil, India, Mexico, and South Africa] for countries like China (i.e. countries currently without commitments under the Kyoto Protocol) to adopt carbon trading as part of their climate policy, and there needs to be an assessment of whether such schemes really work in reducing atmospheric carbon—or if they are simply a means for polluting industries to profitably avoid the issue of making emissions cuts.

Cap-and-Trade

The free-market logic behind the scheme looks simple on paper. Countries taking part in "cap and trade" schemes like the European Union Emissions Trading Scheme (EU-ETS) have a

Kevin Smith, "Carbon Trading: The Limits of Free-Market Logic," *China Dialogue*, September 17, 2007. Reproduced by permission of the author. www.carbontradewatch.org.

limit set on the amount of carbon they can emit in a given time period (the "cap"). This allotted amount of carbon is carved up and allocated between different industrial locations in the country. If, for example, a cement factory goes over its allocated portion of carbon emissions, it has to purchase spare emissions from another market participant, for example, a power station that has emitted less than its allocation, and can therefore sell them profitably on (the "trade").

The problem lies in the fact that carbon trading is designed with the express purpose of providing an opportunity for rich countries to delay making costly, structural changes towards low-carbon technologies. This isn't a malfunction of the market or an unexpected by-product: this is what the market was designed to do. The economist John Kay wrote in the *Financial Times*: "when a market is created through political action rather than emerging spontaneously from the needs of buyers and sellers, business will seek to influence market design for commercial advantage." In terms of climate change and carbon trading, the "commercial advantage" (at least in the short term) lies in avoiding the costly structural changes, and industry has influenced every stage of the design and implementation of the carbon market to this end.

It is much cheaper for industry to purchase cheap carbon credits. . . than to implement the technologies that would actually bring about real emissions reductions.

Businesses and industries in the global north have avoided making these infrastructural changes by ensuring that the price of carbon permits is kept absurdly low. It is much cheaper for industry to purchase cheap carbon credits to make up any emissions short-falls than to implement the technologies that would actually bring about real emissions reductions at source.

The low price of carbon permits was ensured in the first round of the EU-ETS by governments handing many more emissions permits to industry than was necessary; the majority of industrial locations had more emissions permits than they needed. When news of this massive over-allocation was revealed, it caused the price of carbon to drop dramatically. Economists estimate that carbon permits should be priced at around 30 to 50 euros per tonne in order to create sufficient incentives for low-carbon technologies. Towards the end of the first round of the EU-ETS the price of permits was regularly dipping below one euro per tonne.

Market enthusiasts argue that the "cap" will be tightened in the second round, causing the price of carbon to rise. But in order to prevent this happening, business has lobbied for a means of importing more cheap credits into the system, generated in countries like China, through the Clean Development Mechanism.

Clean Development?

Instead of trading with other market participants in Europe, another option for our cement factory would be to purchase "carbon credits" that have been generated outside of the trading scheme, through a project in a developing country that supposedly reduces or avoids emissions. An example would be a hydro-electric power station in China that has sold its supposed emissions reductions to companies from rich countries as part of the Clean Development Mechanism (CDM) [a carbon offset scheme created by the Kyoto Protocol, a treaty to cut greenhouse gas emissions]. China has been the world leader in this market, generating some 60% of all CDM credits in 2006.

The CDM has had some bad publicity in [2008]. . . . An article in *The Guardian* newspaper in June 2007, said: "[the CDM] has been contaminated by gross incompetence, rule-breaking and possible fraud by companies in the developing world, according to UN paperwork, an unpublished expert report and alarming feedback from projects on the ground."

There is both the incentive and the opportunity for [carbon offset] project developers to ... make a project appear more effective and generate more credits.

Despite the regulatory framework that surrounds the CDM, there is both the incentive and the opportunity for project developers to distort key information, so as to make a project appear more effective and generate more credits—or gloss over any local resistance to the project.

For example, the principle of "additionality" is a prerequisite for a project to qualify for CDM status: it has to be proved that the project would not have taken place without the funding provided through the CDM; any climate benefits should be additional as a result of the funding. Otherwise, unscrupulous operators could simply claim carbon funding for projects that would have taken place anyway, meaning industries in rich countries could justify further pollution on the false premise of being responsible for emissions reductions elsewhere.

However, many CDM projects under consideration in China involve generating hydro-electricity: there are 248 currently in the pipeline. There are strong grounds to be extremely sceptical over whether these are genuinely additional, given that such projects are very common in China, and have been actively promoted by the government. The question arises over whether they would have been happening had it not been for CDM funding. In 2005, the International Rivers Network submitted a comment to the CDM panel in reference to the Xiaogushan Large Hydroelectric Project in northwest China's Gansu province, which pointed out that the application for CDM funding was submitted two years after the construction of the dam had begun, and that "project documentation from the Asian Development Bank clearly states that Xiaogushan was the least-cost generation option for Gansu and that revenue from CDM credits was irrelevant to the decision to go ahead with the project."

It is not well documented whether there is local support for the various hydro-electric projects in China that are being promoted through the CDM, which as a pre-requisite should bring developmental benefits to local communities. Many of the corporate benefactors of CDM money in other countries are the target of sustained local resistance from communities who have to endure the often life-threatening impacts of intensive, industrial pollution.

In 2005, about 10,000 people from social movements, community groups and civil society organisations mobilised in Chhattisgarh, India, to protest the environmental public hearing held for the expansion of Jindal Steel and Power Limited (JSPL) sponge iron plants in the district. The production of sponge iron (an impure form of the metal) is notoriously dirty, and companies involved have been accused of land-grabbing, as well as causing intensive air, soil and water pollution. JSPL runs the largest sponge-iron plant in the world, which is spread over 320 hectares on what used to be the thriving, agricultural village of Patrapali. This plant alone has four separate CDM projects, generating millions of tonnes of supposed carbon reductions that could be imported into the EU-ETS. The inhabitants of three surrounding villages that would be engulfed are resisting a proposed 20 billion rupee (around US$412 million) expansion. In this case, the CDM is not only providing financial assistance to JSPL in making the expansion, but also providing them with "green" credibility by putting them at the forefront of the emerging carbon market.

The head of China's environmental agency, Zhou Shengxian, recently attributed the rise in social unrest across the country to pollution scandals and the degradation of the environment. An article in *The Guardian* newspaper said that his comments "underscore the frustration of state mandarins at local government officials who ignore environmental standards in order to attract investment, jobs and bribes." Given such circumstances, it is highly possible that the CDM will provide financial support to the sort of environmentally irresponsible power and chemical plants that are increasingly becoming the target of community protest in China.

The structure of the CDM is such that it is usually an option reserved for large companies who can provide the capital needed . . . to implement the project.

Pollution and Power

The largest share of CDM credits worldwide (30%) has been generated by the destruction of HFC-23 [trifluoromethane]. This potent greenhouse gas is created by the manufacture of refrigerant gases. A study in the February 2007 article of *Nature* showed that the value of these credits at current carbon prices was 4.7 billion euros. Not only was this twice the value of the refrigerant gases themselves, but it was also estimated that the cost of implementing the necessary technology to capture and destroy the HFC-23 was less than 100 million euros: something in the region of 4.6 billion euros was being generated in profit for the owners of the plants and the project brokers. In an article in the *Sunday Times*, it was reported that two Chinese companies were set to make around US$1 billion in 2007 alone as a result of CDM money given for the destruction of HFC-23.

This enormous sum of money generated by these Kyoto-style trading schemes has not gone to the companies and communities who are taking action on clean energy and energy-reduction projects, but rather to big, industrial polluters who are then at liberty to reinvest the profits into the expansion of their operations. Ashish Bharat Ram, the managing director of an Indian company that reported a profit of 87 million euros from the destruction of HFC-23 in 2006 and 2007, told the *Economic Times* that: "Strong income from carbon trading strengthened us financially, and now we are expanding into areas related to our core strength of chemical and technical textiles business."

It seems that the only people who are benefiting from the carbon market and CDM projects are the polluting corporations.

The structure of the CDM is such that it is usually an option reserved for large companies who can provide the capital needed not only to implement the project, but also to go through the long process of accreditation and certification, with all the attendant expenses of carbon consultants, third-party verifiers, ongoing project monitoring and so forth. Larry Lohmann argues in his book *Carbon Trading—A Critical Conversation on Climate Change, Privatisation and Power* that this "reinforces a system in which, ironically, the main entities recognized as being capable of making 'emissions reductions' are the corporations most committed to a fossil-fuel burning future. . . while indigenous communities, environmental movements and ordinary people acting more constructively to tackle climate change are tacitly excluded, their creativity unrecognized, and their claims suppressed."

It seems that the only people who are benefiting from the carbon market and CDM projects are the polluting corporations that are involved in both Europe and the global south as the new class of handsomely-salaried carbon technocrats and brokers, which has sprung up to service the needs of the market. There is an urgent need to recognise that the market's fixation on short-term profit maximisation is not an appropriate instrument to induce the large-scale and costly infrastructural changes that need to take place in all countries in the transition to low-carbon economies.

Many Carbon Offset Projects Have a Negative Impact on the Environment and Global Warming

Wouter Buytaert

Wouter Buytaert is a postdoctoral researcher in the Department of Environmental Science at Lancaster University in the United Kingdom.

A t this year's [2007] European Geosciences Union (EGU) meeting, we challenged the scientific community to think about the carbon footprint of academic travel. This action resulted in a healthy debate about the environmental and social benefit of scientific conferences. One of the recurrent suggestions for concrete action was that the EGU should incorporate the cost of buying carbon credits in the meeting registration fee. The idea is to offset the carbon emissions of the event, including travel, and so to make the conference carbon neutral. However, carbon offset schemes are controversial in their own right and may be worth a scientific debate of their own. Here I highlight some reasons why we should be cautious.

Effectiveness of Reforestation Projects

A first concern is the effectiveness of carbon offset schemes. Increasing environmental awareness among companies and individuals has sparked an emerging and lucrative market in carbon credits based on a plethora of carbon reduction projects. But due to a shortage of verification, the impact of these actions may be questioned. Some practices are inherently flawed, such as preventing clearcutting of forests that would be preserved for conservation anyway, or selling credits

Wouter Buytaert, "Talking Point: Carbon Offset Schemes Are of Questionable Value," environmentalresearchweb.org, June 12, 2007. Reproduced by permission.

for cleaner and more efficient production techniques that are introduced for economic reasons. Other practices fail because of insufficient scientific understanding of the system.

For instance, (re)forestation in developing countries is one of the most popular offset schemes. Forests are a convenient method of capturing and storing atmospheric carbon. There are also several positive side effects. Many forests, in particular where native species are used, are a breeding ground for biodiversity. Forests may be planted on degraded areas and reduce erosion, and they may also provide a sustainable source of firewood and other environmental services for local inhabitants.

(Re)forestation in developing countries is one of the most popular offset schemes. Forests are a convenient method of capturing and storing atmospheric carbon.

But there are negative side effects too. Carbon offset schemes tend to focus on fast-growing trees, such as eucalyptus and pine, which are non-native and have a far lower environmental and biodiversity benefit than native species. Tree plantations also tend to consume more water than grasses and shrubs. On a global scale, tree plantations decrease streamflow by about 200 mm per year (roughly 50%). This may have serious impacts on the local water cycle. For instance, extensive parts of the Andean páramo [a high altitude ecosystem] have been forested with pine for carbon sequestration purposes. The páramo is an ecosystem that consists of extensive grasslands in the upper parts of the tropical Andes, and stores vast amounts of water in its soils, swamps and lakes. It provides many environmental functions, but the most important is water supply for the highland area, including major cities such as Bogotá, Colombia, and Quito, Ecuador. Forestation with pine reduces streamflow by about 70%. Since most of this reduction affects low flow conditions, the consequences for local water security are serious.

What's more, the higher water consumption of pine may even result in a net carbon release to the atmosphere. Páramo wetlands store high amounts of organic carbon. This accumulation of organic matter is strongly linked to water saturation of the soils for large periods of the year. Dessication of the soils after forestation induces faster organic matter decomposition, which may offset carbon storage in the biomass aboveground. In Indonesia, the conversion of peat bogs into oil palm plantations has had similar effects.

Forestation activities in the Andes now focus more on biodiversity and use indigenous [tree] species such as Polylepis. However, there is no scientific consensus about the historical vegetation patterns of the páramo. What is considered reforestation may well be forestation of valuable and original grassland ecosystems. And since the impact of those forests on the local water cycle is not well understood, care should be taken not to disrupt a delicate and valuable hydrological system.

Our current carbon footprint is too high, and the only long-term solution is to reduce carbon emissions, not to compensate them by carbon offset schemes.

Sustainability Concerns

Even if such scientific questions are solved, significant concerns remain about the sustainability of carbon pools in forests. Forests capture most carbon early in their life cycle. The biomass of a mature forest is nearly stable, and organic carbon capture can only be maintained if carbon is transferred to another sink, such as the soil. As this is not always the case, organic carbon capture can only continue if both the current forest is maintained and even more area is forested. Although this may seem preferable from an environmentalist viewpoint, it is not sustainable in the long term.

This lack of sustainability points to the essence of the problem. Our current carbon footprint is too high, and the only long-term solution is to reduce carbon emissions, not to compensate them by carbon offset schemes. This is also why carbon offset schemes are opposed from an ethical viewpoint. They are considered as paying someone else for reducing their greenhouse gas emissions and, as such, buying your way out of responsibility. And the schemes may distract attention from the real problem of how we reduce our own emissions. This is a double challenge for scientists. Finding new ways to decrease our society's greenhouse gas emissions is a major scientific challenge that merits our full attention. Considering whether the scientific value of a trip to the other end of the world out-weighs the use of resources and the carbon footprint is a much more personal challenge.

Individual Carbon Offsets Simply Allow the Rich to Ease Their Guilt Without Changing Their Lifestyles

Robert Frank

Robert Frank is a senior writer for the Wall Street Journal, *an English-language international daily newspaper published by Dow Jones & Company in New York City.*

It's not easy being green—especially if you're rich.

With their growing fleets of yachts, jets and cars, and their sprawling estates, today's outsized wealthy have also become outsized polluters. There are now 10,000 private jets swarming American skies, all burning more than 15 times as much fuel per passenger as commercial planes. The summer seas are increasingly crowded with megayachts swallowing up to 80 gallons of fuel an hour.

With the green movement in vogue, the rich are looking for ways to compensate for their carbon-dioxide generation . . . without crimping their style.

Yet with the green movement in vogue, the rich are looking for ways to compensate for their carbon-dioxide generation, which is linked to global warming, without crimping their style. Some are buying carbon "offsets" for their private-jet flights, which help fund alternate-energy technologies such as windmills, or carbon dioxide-eating greenery such as trees.

Others are installing ocean-monitoring equipment on their yachts. And a few are building green-certified mansions, complete with solar-heated indoor swimming pools.

The Debate About Carbon Offsets

Some people say the measures are a noble effort on the part of the wealthy to improve the environment. Eric Carlson, executive director and founder of the Carbon Fund, a nonprofit that works with companies and individuals to offset emissions, says the wealthy are taking the lead in alternative-energy markets such as solar technologies just as they take the lead in consumer markets.

"Obviously these people have different lifestyles from yours or mine," Mr. Carlson says. "At the same time, they're not obligated to do anything. We praise those who are doing things. We're trying to get to a market where the superwealthy are leaders in reducing their [carbon dioxide] footprint and playing a major role in changing this market."

Environmentalists say that if the rich really wanted to help the environment, they would stop flying on private jets, live in smaller homes, and buy kayaks instead of yachts.

Others say the efforts are little more than window-dressing, designed to ease the guilt of the wealthy or boost their status among an increasingly green elite. Environmentalists say that if the rich really wanted to help the environment, they would stop flying on private jets, live in smaller homes, and buy kayaks instead of yachts.

"Carbon offsets and these other things are feel-good solutions," says Lester Brown, founder and president of the Earth Policy Institute [an environmental organization]. "I'm always interested in people who buy a carbon offset for their jet to fly between their four big homes. These kinds of programs postpone more meaningful action."

Companies Offering Offsets

Either way, an increasing number of companies are launching programs designed to help the rich live large while staying green. Jets.com, a private jet service, plans to start a program in early September [2007] in partnership with the Carbon Fund [a provider of carbon offsets]. After they take a trip, customers will get a statement on their bills telling them how much carbon dioxide their flight emitted and what it would cost to buy offsets from the fund.

The offsets are a bargain compared with the flights: A round-trip private-jet flight between Fort Lauderdale, Fla., and Boston costs about $20,000. The offsets for the 13 metric tons of carbon dioxide emitted would cost about $74, the company says.

V1 Jets International, a jet charter company, rolled out its "Green Card" program that it says accentuates "the positive effect your flight emissions will have on the environment." The company calculates the total emissions from the trip and then buys a carbon offset from the Carbon Fund. "From a jet perspective, we have a responsibility to look after the damage that these planes do," says Andrew Zarrow, V1's president. The company also has created technologies designed to make flights more efficient by selling seats on "deadleg" trips—flights that are returning empty from one-way trips.

Yacht companies also are getting into the act. Trinity Yachts, a Gulfport, Miss., builder, this month announced it will pay for part of the cost of installing special oceanographic and atmospheric monitoring systems in all of its new boats.

The system, called the SeaKeeper 1000, measures water temperatures and salinity, as well as air temperature and wind speed. The data are sent to scientists who monitor the earth's oceans. Trinity's program is in partnership with International

Sea-Keepers, a nonprofit marine conservation group founded by a group of yacht owners concerned about the environment.

"The caliber of client we have is very aware of what's going on in the environment," says William S. Smith III, vice president of Trinity Yachts. Still, the system doesn't reduce emissions from the yachts themselves, which can burn hundreds of gallons of fuel a day.

Green Houses

Some wealthy people are going green with their houses, too. The U.S. Green Building Council has certified at least three mansions for being leaders in environmental design, including one owned by Ted Turner's daughter, Laura Turner Seydel, and her husband, Rutherford, in Atlanta. The 7,000-square-foot-plus house, called EcoManor, is equipped with 27 photovoltaic panels on the roof, rainwater-collecting tanks for supplying toilet water, and "gray water" systems that use water from the showers and sinks for the lawn and gardens. The top of the house is insulated with a soy-based foam that is more efficient than fiberglass. The home has 40 energy monitors and a switch near the door that turns off every light in the house before the family leaves.

Mr. Seydel says the couple's energy bill is about half that of comparable homes. While he acknowledges they could have built a slightly smaller house, he said all the space is well used, between kids and visiting friends and in-laws.

"The wealthy have always been the early adapters to technology," he says. "I'm hoping that we can pave the way and show that you can have something that's luxurious that also makes a lot of sense from an energy and convenience point of view."

CHAPTER 3

Are Tree-Based Carbon Offsets Beneficial?

Chapter Overview

Toni Johnson

Toni Johnson is a staff writer for the Council on Foreign Relations, a foreign-policy think tank.

Loss of forests contributes as much as 30 percent of global greenhouse-gas emissions each year—rivaling emissions from the global transportation sector. The Kyoto Protocol's [an international treaty to cut greenhouse gas emissions] offset mechanisms ... allow credits to be given for replanting trees or establishing new forests, which capture carbon dioxide through photosynthesis. But the current policy regimen does nothing to prevent existing forests from being cut down in the first place. With Kyoto set to expire in 2012, a new round of talks is under way to develop the next framework for climate change. Experts believe a policy to avoid further deforestation will be a major topic at the conference. But some environmentalists remain wary of forestry climate policy, fearing it will draw attention away from the need to reduce emissions caused by fossil fuels.

The State of Global Forests and Deforestation

The world currently has about ten billion acres of forest. According to the UN [United Nations] Food and Agriculture Organization's (FAO) 2007 report on the world's forests, the world lost about 3 percent of forest area between 1990 and 2005, and the net rate of loss has declined since 2000 (the world loses on average 32 million acres per year). Growth in northern hemisphere forest has helped offset tropical deforestation. There is disagreement, however, on the extent to which increases in temperate-zone forests offset the loss of carbon sinking in tropical zones.

Deforestation is caused by exploitation of natural resources—including expanding populations, logging, agriculture, biofuel production, and wildfires. Clearing forests for the production of biofuels is causing major concern, as experts contend that it has a significant negative impact on forests without doing much to reduce greenhouse gas emissions.

The FAO report shows that the greatest overall loss is occurring in Africa, followed closely by Latin America and the Caribbean. Indonesia has the fastest deforestation rate of any single country in the world. When emissions from loss of forests are taken into account, Indonesia could be considered the world's third-largest emitter of greenhouse gases, according to a recent World Bank report. Indonesia recently has made a show of planting 80 million trees ahead of the Bali conference, but some question the country's long-term commitment to slowing exploitation of its valuable resources, such as stemming illegal logging.

U.S. forests absorb between one million and three million metric tons of carbon dioxide each year.

China's rapid growth in the production of manufactured goods that need wood also poses challenges. The country's consumption of forest products leads the world. According to Forest Trends, a nonprofit research group, China's increasing demand has lead to unsustainable and sometimes illegal logging practices in many of the countries seeing significant deforesting activities, such as Indonesia and Papua New Guinea. "China has a seemingly limitless appetite for cheap wood," says Don J. Melnick, a conservation biology professor at Columbia University. Products made from this timber often wind up in U.S. and European markets. Richard Z. Donovan, chief of forestry for the Rainforest Alliance, an advocacy group, says that right now China is not only adding to climate change by burning large amounts of fossil fuels that emit greenhouse gas but also by being a "non-discriminating buyer" of wood.

Forests: A Vital Part of the Solution

Trees capture carbon dioxide by taking it into their cells through photosynthesis. They then store the carbon in their bodies; a tree is comprised of about 50 percent carbon. Some carbon gets released back into the atmosphere through respiration, but the net effect is tremendous carbon storage. The Union of Concerned Scientists estimates that U.S. forests absorb between one million and three million metric tons of carbon dioxide each year, perhaps offsetting between 20 percent and 46 percent of the country's greenhouse-gas emissions.

When trees are burned, harvested, or otherwise die, they release their carbon back into the atmosphere. The 2007 forest fires in the United States, for example, are estimated to account for between 4 percent and 6 percent of North American greenhouse-gas emissions for the year. Some environmental experts believe climate change may be a contributor to decreasing rainfall in some areas, thus increasing the likelihood of wildfires.

The offset mechanisms set up by the UN's Kyoto Protocol allow . . . reforestation (forest restoration) and afforestation (the planting of new forests) projects . . . [but not] deforestation.

Carbon Offsets from Forestry

The offset mechanisms set up by the UN's Kyoto Protocol allow a small fraction of the total credits each country is allocated for offsetting greenhouse-gas emissions to come from reforestation (forest restoration) and afforestation (the planting of new forests) projects. None are allowed for deforestation. To date, out of about 860 projects registered worldwide, only one project located in China has made it through the entire Kyoto process (others are at various interim stages). The process for getting a registered project is complex and expensive. "The reality is that very few local communities have the capacity to maneuver through the process," says Celia A. Harvey, senior adviser for forest carbon projects at Conservation International, an environmental advocacy group. These credits also are set to expire after a few years, which makes them less profitable than other Kyoto offsets, experts say.

One requirement of the UN credits mechanism presents particular difficulties for forestry projects. Roger A. Sedjo, a forestry expert for Resources for the Future, an environmental think tank, says Kyoto's "additionality" requirement—proof that project emissions outcomes would not have occurred without intervention—encourages "crummy projects" that are less effective and difficult to approve. It is extremely difficult to prove that these emissions reductions would not have occurred anyway.

Other environmentalists are concerned that forestry projects will lead to less biodiversity and an erosion of rights for indigenous forest dwellers.

Reservations About Forest Carbon Sinking

Some environmental advocates remain cautious about including forest management in climate-change protocols because they worry it will distract from mitigating emissions caused by fossil fuels. Others worry that forest carbon sinking is difficult to monitor. Still others are concerned that the logistics of compensating people for not doing something is problematic. Projects are by jeopardized by forest fires, bug infestations and diseases, illegal logging, and even human malice. The European emissions trading scheme, for example, does not give credits to forestry projects, in part because of such concerns. Forest projects, however, are beginning to generate credits sold on the Chicago Climate Exchange, a voluntary carbon market.

Other environmentalists are concerned that forestry projects will lead to less biodiversity and an erosion of rights for indigenous forest dwellers. In Uganda, for example, a re-foresting project became embroiled in a battle over land access between the government and local farmers living at the forest's edge. Donovan says the best way to prevent such problems is to make sure indigenous groups are allowed to participate in negotiations on policy for their area.

Without avoided deforestation, some experts say that efforts to reduce greenhouse gas from other sectors will be more expensive and take twice as long.

On biodiversity, Harvey notes that the majority of forestry projects so far have focused on fast-growing, mono-species plantations. These trees present known quantities for growing and carbon measurements, making them more attractive projects, while native trees have potential that still needs to be assessed. Donovan argues that allowing plantation projects to be included in the Kyoto process may have provided a "perverse incentive" to cut down existing forests in order to have the opportunity to replant them. Both Harvey and Donovan agree the first priority should be to conserve current forests, which provide more benefits than just carbon mitigation, such as protecting natural habitats.

Currently, "avoided deforestation" remains outside the climate policy mix. But without avoided deforestation, some experts say that efforts to reduce greenhouse gas from other sectors will be more expensive and take twice as long. Some experts believe that deforestation rates in Indonesia and Brazil alone are enough to undo 80 percent of the emissions reductions designated under the Kyoto Protocol. Experts also say avoided deforestation is a less expensive option for reducing emissions when compared to options such as upgrading power plants.

Forestry and Future Climate Change Policy

Lowering deforestation has become a high priority and is expected to figure prominently in discussions on the next international framework for climate change. The 2007 climate change conference in Bali [Indonesia] yielded an agreement to include deforestation and greater forest management in the next climate change protocol. The agreement also allows deforestation efforts and incentives to be started under the current Kyoto regime ahead of any new protocol.

Lowering deforestation has become a high priority and is expected to figure prominently in discussions on the next international framework for climate change.

An Intergovernmental Panel on Climate Change (IPCC) report points out that the most sustainable policy for use of forestry as a climate-change tool is one that maintains or increases forest carbon stock while sustaining timber yields. That means slowing the rate for deforestation while providing enough timber and agricultural land to meet the world's growing appetite. Cutting deforestation rates by 50 percent over the next century would provide about 12 percent of the emissions reductions needed to keep carbon dioxide concentrations to 450 parts per million, a goal the IPCC argues is necessary to prevent significant increases in global temperatures. Experts predict that ahead of any final policy on avoided deforestation, more projects will begin trading on the voluntary market, similar to what happened before the Kyoto Protocol went into its enforcement period.

Experts point out a successful deforestation program lies in its design. Two major "flash points" will complicate the deforestation policy debate—accounting for emissions reductions and paying for conservation. Some advocates would like to see emissions-reduction accounting by project, while others believe the only way to prevent deforestation from moving outside project areas is to account for emissions reductions countrywide. Experts say the assumption is that deforestation efforts will join the credit-trading system already under way. However, some people are pushing for a fund that governments would pay into for designated forest conservation. Melnick notes that a fund would be less effective than a market-based mechanism because governments would never put enough money into the fund. "We can't get money into funds for starving children and people with AIDS," Melnick argues. "So getting money for trees is complete fantasy." In a CFR.org Podcast, Joshua Busby, an expert on climate change politics, also notes there is debate about whether avoided deforestation monies will be dispersed to governments, large corporations or local communities.

With carbon credits selling at about twenty dollars per ton on the European market, experts say a market-based mechanism would provide enough incentive to avoid deforestation. Donovan says timber and agriculture opportunities from forest land often provide less than a dollar per acre. One exception may be biofuel production; as costs for ethanol increase, experts expect to see greater pressure on forests, even with market credits in place. And some people worry that adding deforestation credits to the market will depress current carbon prices, although others note that plans to expand emissions caps to more industry sectors and the possible inclusion of the United States may increase the need for credits.

Other issues also need attention, such as reducing the complexity of the UN's project accrediting system to open it up to more people. Another issue is whether avoided deforestation will be included within the current UN mechanisms or if a new type of mechanism will be created. Setting baselines—how much emissions reductions—for avoided deforestation projects also need to be decided. And some people are pushing for carbon sequestration from wood products, such as furniture, to be included. But Harvey contends that may be too complex.

Carbon Credits Can Encourage Developing Nations to Protect Trees

Rachel Oliver

Rachel Oliver is a reporter and project coordinator at CNN.com, *an international news and information Web site based in Atlanta, Georgia.*

Cutting down trees is pretty much one of the worst things you can do when it comes to climate change. Deforestation, by varying accounts, contributes anywhere from 20 percent to 30 percent of all carbon dioxide (CO_2) emissions—around 1.6 billion tons.

When you cut down trees you get a double whammy. First of all, they are not called the lungs of the Earth for nothing—we clearly need trees so that we and other animals can breathe. Trees also are in the front line against pollution, breathing in millions of tons of greenhouse gases a year that they store in their trunks.

According to the United Nations' Environmental Programme (UNEP), trees store a staggering 283 gigatons of carbon in their biomass. When that is combined with the carbon found in the surrounding deadwood and soil, the result is 50 percent more carbon than is currently found in the atmosphere. When those trees are felled or burned—trees that are comprised of 50 percent carbon—that carbon is then released into the atmosphere.

According to the Council of Foreign Relations, the 2007 forest fires in the United States—a relatively minor incident on a global scale—contributed as much as 6 percent of North America's total greenhouse gas emissions that year.

Rachel Oliver, "All About: Forests and Carbon Trading," *CNN.com*, February 11, 2008. www.cnn.com. Reproduced by permission.

But burning trees isn't always a phenomena directly controlled by humans. Many believe that global warming is exacerbating the rate of naturally occurring forest fires around the world.

"Natural variation suggests the Amazon should have serious drought-led fires at 400- to 700-year intervals, but today, they are happening every five to 15 years," the *Independent* [a British daily newspaper] recently reported. "It's a vicious cycle: cutting back the forests causes more global warming, which then burns up more forests, which causes more global warming, which burns up the forests even more, and on and on."

There are currently around 10 billion acres of forest in the world, covering 30 percent of the Earth's land area. The world's forest cover is at least one-third less of the size it was before the earliest days of agriculture.

Around 32 million acres of forests disappear every year, most of it in the tropics.

Nations Consider 'Carbon Trading'

According to the U.N.'s [United Nations] Food and Agricultural Organisation (FAO), around 32 million acres of forests disappear every year, most of it in the tropics. The main reason for forest clearing hasn't changed in 10,000 years. As much as 80 percent of all deforestation is done because of the need to clear land for agriculture. The WWF [World Wildlife Fund, an environmental organization] is now warning that if nothing is done 60 percent of the Amazon rain forest could disappear by 2030.

A recent UK [United Kingdom] study on the environment, the *Stern Report*, reached the conclusion that many others are coming to: If the world wants to curb emissions cheaply and quickly then it has to simply stop cutting down so many trees.

One way to do this is to make it more economically viable for the countries hosting these rain forests to preserve them.

Carbon trading was introduced as part of the Kyoto Protocol's [an international treaty to cut greenhouse gas emissions] goal to reduce certain industrial nations' greenhouse gas emissions to below 1990 levels by 2012. The idea was that countries whose emissions fall under the emissions cap—the permitted level of CO_2 equivalent emissions per year—could then sell those carbon credits to countries who are not able to meet their own caps.

The idea [with carbon trading] . . . [is that] countries (generally poor ones) who have the rain forests should be compensated for protecting them.

The caps are supposed to fall over time with the price of the carbon credits, therefore rising due to scarcity levels. Proponents of carbon trading envisage a new global investment market based on emissions trading, where companies and countries have incentives to invest in developing world projects due to the highly coveted carbon credits they receive for doing so.

With regard to forests, the idea is basically they should be worth more than they are. And countries (generally poor ones) who have the rain forests should be compensated for protecting them, particularly when they are under so much economic pressure to open them up to mining companies. Indonesia and Brazil now find themselves in the top four of the world's top polluting nations as a result (around 80 percent of Brazil's greenhouse gas emissions tally comes from deforestation).

The economic argument goes that you make it more financially appealing to countries not to allow their forests to be cut down.

"It's insanity that a single service company, Google, has a market value of $200 billion, while all the services of all of the world's great forests are valued at nothing," Hylton Murray-Philipson, head of Rainforest Concern, recently told the *Independent* newspaper.

On a per ton of carbon basis, countries such as Indonesia can earn between $1 and $5 to destroy the trees, according to a recent article in the *Guardian* [a British newspaper]—or they can earn around $30 (the market price of carbon credits in Europe at the time the article was written) for protecting them. Equally, a 2006 study on deforestation by the British government said that without action on this issue, each ton emitted could cause $85 of damage to the global economy.

The real concern . . . is that carbon trading only really serves rich nations [and] . . . could put the vital resources of the developing world in the hands of [those] nations.

Can Interests of Both Rich, Poor Be Served?

The real concern, however, is that carbon trading only really serves rich nations; the issue being that carbon trading could put the vital resources of the developing world in the hands of nations that can use carbon credits as a way to counter, or delay, reductions of their own greenhouse gas emissions at the same time.

At the U.N. climate change conference held last December in Bali, Indonesia, the World Bank launched its Forest Carbon Partnership Facility (FCPF), a fund financed by the UK, Germany, the Netherlands, Australia, Japan, France, Switzerland, Denmark and Finland (with The Nature Conservancy also chipping in).

The $160 million fund, the World Bank says, will be used to "support programs targeting the drivers of deforestation and develop concrete activities to reach out to poor people who depend on forests to improve their livelihoods. It will also help developing countries build the technical, regulatory, and sustainable forestry capacity to reduce emissions from deforestation and degradation."

There has already been some confusion over the exact role the World Bank is trying to play in all of this. The World Bank says it wants to reduce global deforestation by 10 percent by 2010. But its critics claim the World Bank has traditionally been a proponent of deforestation.

There has also been concern over the impact of the forest carbon trading scheme on local forest communities that earn a living from the forests.

In the Democratic Republic of Congo (DRC) the World Bank is facing opposition from Pygmy groups [a tribal group in Africa] and local communities which rely on the Congo basin, the world's second-largest virgin rain forest, for their livelihoods, following a leaked report on the Bank's activities there. The report came from the Bank's own inspection panel, and it accused the Bank of encouraging commercial logging practices "based on exaggerated estimates of the export revenue to be reaped," while discouraging sustainable forestry and conservation at the same time, reports the Inter Press Service.

The report has also found that the financial benefits of logging have gone to foreign firms, not local ones. The Pygmy groups and others are asking for these industrial logging practices to stop immediately and are asking for more assessments of the environmental impact of logging. (Logging was actually banned in DRC back in 2002; since then more than 100 new logging contracts have been issued).

Environmental groups have responded to the World Bank's FCPF with extreme caution. A joint statement signed by more than 80 environmental organizations around the world in response to the program queried its intentions, accusing the

Bank of continuing "to undermine its own climate change mitigation efforts by persisting in funding fossil fuel industries on a global scale and enabling deforestation."

They have also sounded their alarm about why the program has been pushed through too quickly with little consultation with affected communities.

Carbon Credits Could Save the Rainforests

Rhett A. Butler

Rhett A. Butler lives in San Francisco and is the founder of Mongabay.com, a Web site concerned with saving the world's rainforests.

A new rainforest conservation initiative by developing nations offers great promise to help slow tropical deforestation rates says William Laurance, a leading rainforest biologist from the Smithsonian Tropical Research Institute in Panama, in an article appearing Friday [April 2006] in *New Scientist*.

Laurance, who is also president of the Association for Tropical Biology and Conservation, says the proposal "basically involves selling or renting rainforests to help protect the billions of tons of carbon they store, thereby slowing the rapid buildup of carbon dioxide and other greenhouse gases in the atmosphere."

Carbon Credits for Slowing Deforestation

The new initiative, proposed by an alliance of ten developing countries led by Papua New Guinea, would establish a mechanism by which industrialized countries would compensate tropical countries for the services rainforests provide the rest of the world, focusing initially on carbon sequestration by forests. Forests play an important role in the carbon cycle. As forests grow, they absorb atmospheric carbon into their tissues via photosynthesis. The opposite occurs when they are cut, thinned and degraded: carbon is released into the atmosphere, contributing to global warming. The U.N. [United Nations] estimates that 20–25 percent of greenhouse gas emissions come from the destruction and degradation of forests, an amount similar to the volume produced each year by the United States.

Tropical forests have the best potential for mitigating rising concentrations of greenhouse gases since they have the greatest capacity to store carbon in their tissues as they grow. Some experts estimate that the reforestation of 3.9 million square miles (10 million square km) could sequester 100–150 billion metric tons of carbon dioxide over the next 50–100 years.

The new initiative ... would establish a mechanism by which industrialized countries would compensate tropical countries for the services rainforests provide.

Under the proposed scheme, in helping developing countries slow deforestation, industrial nations would earn 'carbon credits' that would count toward their emissions targets under the Kyoto Protocol or other international agreements.

"It's potentially a win-win situation for everybody involved," said Laurance. "The forests win, the atmosphere wins, the international community wins, and developing nations struggling to overcome poverty win."

Tropical forests have the best potential for mitigating rising concentrations of greenhouse gases since they have the greatest capacity to store carbon.

"Of course, the devil is in the details," Laurance admits. He notes that "earlier efforts to establish rainforest-carbon trading under Kyoto were defeated, in part because countries couldn't agree about whether and how to credit countries that slowed forest destruction."

Nevertheless, the Coalition for Rainforest Nations' proposal is gaining ground. In December 2005 at the United Nations Framework Convention on Climate Change in Montreal, the U.N. agreed in principal to support the initiative and even the U.S., which initially opposed the proposal, expressed interest.

High Stakes

A lot is at stake for developing countries. Focusing specifically on the value of carbon sequestration the coalition could be talking a lot of money. At the current going rate of $20 for a one-ton unit of carbon dioxide, the forests of Bolivia, Central African Republic, Chile, Congo, Costa Rica, Democratic Republic of Congo, the Dominican Republic, Guatemala, Nicaragua, and Papua New Guinea (coalition members) are worth around $1.1 trillion for their carbon sequestration alone. Of course the forests offer a great deal more value through the other, less measurable services they provide including fisheries protection, biodiversity preservation, erosion and flood control, recreation and tourism value, harvest of renewable products, and water services.

For comparison, a recent study by the Pembina Institute for the Canadian Boreal Initiative found that carbon stored in Canada's boreal forests and peatlands is worth $3.7 trillion, while the annual value of ecosystem services like water filtration, pest-control services, and carbon storage at $93 billion—roughly 2.5 times greater than the net market value of forestry, hydroelectric, mining, and oil and gas extraction in Canada's Boreal region. The values can be expected to be similar in tropical countries.

Deforestation of tropical rainforests has a global impact through species extinction, the loss of important ecosystem services and renewable resources, and the reduction of carbon sinks. Recently a study by NASA [National Aeronautics and Space Administration] found a direct impact that tropical deforestation has on the economies of the United States and Europe. Research shows that deforestation in the Amazon region of South America influences rainfall from Mexico to Texas and in the Gulf of Mexico, while forest loss in Central Africa affects precipitation patterns in the upper and lower U.S. Midwest. Similarly, deforestation in Southeast Asia was found to influence rainfall in China and the Balkan Peninsula.

Many Hurdles Ahead

While the potential benefits seem clear, no one expects that implementing the proposal will be simple.

"There are still many hurdles to clear," said Laurance. "But a key point is that, if a viable rainforest-carbon trading mechanism is established, the perverse economic logic that currently drives rapid forest destruction could be profoundly altered. That would make us all breathe a little easier."

Should the initiative come into being, it is likely that it would include provisions for the restoration of degraded forests and the development of plantations on deforested lands. Tropical countries would then have an incentive to begin replanting the forests that have so rapidly been lost due to logging, commercial and subsistence agriculture, and other forms of development over the past 50 years. Already, private companies are positioning themselves to cash in on the potential windfall. Several firms, including Carbon Capital in London, are forming trading partnerships with developing countries, while others are establishing plantations in tropics.

The nascent carbon trading market could prove to be a model for financing large-scale conservation while simultaneously providing profit opportunities for private firms. While corporations pursuing commercial interests could end up doing a lot of good for the global environment, poor countries could have a new way to capitalize on their natural assets without destroying them.

Carbon Offsets for Preventing Deforestation Could Raise the Value of Living Forests

Science Daily

Science Daily is a leading online magazine and Web portal devoted to science, technology, and medicine. The following viewpoint was adapted from materials provided by Consultative Group on International Agriculture Research.

Deforestation in tropical countries is often driven by the perverse economic reality that forests are worth more dead than alive. But a new study by an international consortium of researchers has found that the emerging market for carbon credits has the potential to radically alter that equation.

The study, which was released this week [December 2007] at UNFCC [United Nations Framework Convention on Climate Change] Conference of Parties (COP-13) in Bali, compared the financial gains generated by deforestation over the last 10 to 20 years in areas of Southeast Asia, Central Africa and the Amazon Basin—most of it driven by a desire for farm land or timber—to the amount of carbon that was released by the destruction. That comparison has become critically important because many industries in developed countries are set to spend billions of dollars to meet new requirements for curbing greenhouse gases by purchasing carbon "credits" tied to reductions elsewhere.

The study was conducted by the World Agroforestry Center (ICRAF), the Center for International Forestry Research (CIFOR), the International Center for Tropical Agriculture

(CIAT), and the International Institute for Tropical Agriculture (IITA), four of the 15 centers of the Consultative Group on International Agricultural Research (CGIAR) [a group working to promote sustainable agriculture], and their national partners.

Deforestation in tropical countries is often driven by the perverse economic reality that forests are worth more dead than alive.

The researchers—who conducted the study under the Partnership for Tropical Forest Margins (ASB)—found that in most areas studied, the various ventures that prompted deforestation rarely generated more than $5 for every ton of carbon they released and frequently returned far less than US $1. Meanwhile, European buyers are currently paying 23 euros—about US $35—for an offset tied to a one-ton reduction in carbon.

"Deforestation is almost always driven by a rational response to what the market values and for some time now, it has just made more financial sense to many people in forested areas to cut down the trees," said Brent Swallow, leader of the study and Global Coordinator of the Partnership for Tropical Forest Margins. "What we discovered is that returns for deforestation are generally so paltry that if farmers and other land users were rewarded for the carbon stored in their trees and forests, it is highly likely that a large amount of deforestation and carbon emissions would be prevented."

Developing new incentives for reducing carbon emissions stemming from deforestation is high on the agenda in Bali. Deforestation is rampant in places like Indonesia, the Amazon and the Congo. Currently, confusion over how to value and monitor the large amounts of carbon stored in tropical forests has prevented the inclusion of forests in the carbon offset market that is mainly dominated by reductions achieved in the industrial sector, even though deforestation is responsible for some 20 percent of the world's carbon emissions.

"We understand that allowing people in forested regions of developing countries to participate in carbon markets presents major challenges, but it's naive to think that conservation is going to occur absent a market incentive," said Meine van Noordwijk, Southeast Asia Regional Coordinator of the World Agroforestry Centre (known by its acronym ICRAF). "Everyone has a stake in finding a way to make it work because it's hard to see how any global effort to combat climate change will succeed if it ignores a major source of the problem."

Confusion over how to value and monitor the large amounts of carbon stored in tropical forests has prevented the inclusion of forests in the carbon offset market.

Van Noordwijk and his colleagues arrived at their conclusions on the economics of deforestation after examining the trade-offs between carbon and financial returns in three areas in Indonesia, and one area each in Peru and Cameroon, all of which have undergone extensive deforestation.

They found that in most instances at the sites in Indonesia, deforestation returned less than $5 per ton of carbon released and in some areas, less than $1. For example, in forested areas rich in peat, which is particularly efficient at trapping carbon, the figure was about $0.10 to $0.20 per ton.

Meanwhile, an analysis of deforestation in the Amazonian forests of the Ucayali Province of Peru produced similar results. Most of the deforestation, which was mainly driven by a desire for crop land, generated less than US $5 per ton of carbon released. The Cameroon study sites produced a better return. Deforestation returns about US $11 per ton of carbon emissions, which is mainly due to an increase in secondary forest and the fact that in Cameroon, cocoa production—which elsewhere has decimated tropical forests—has tended to occur within forests, and resulted in more in forest degradation than outright deforestation.

Despite the clear benefits to be derived from assigning carbon credits to conserving forests, implementing a forest-based carbon market will be complicated.

The report notes that offering rewards for carbon storage could be effective not only at encouraging conservation but also at encouraging activities in deforested areas that can recoup at least some of the lost carbon. For example, research shows that agroforestry, which encourages a broader use of trees on farms, can offer a win-win situation of improving smallholder incomes and absorbing carbon.

Dennis Garrity, Director General of the Nairobi, Kenya-based World Agroforestry Centre said that, "Not only does agroforestry have the potential to store carbon, it also addresses the need for alternative livelihoods amongst populations who currently benefit from deforestation."

Researchers caution that despite the clear benefits to be derived from assigning carbon credits to conserving forests, implementing a forest-based carbon market will be complicated.

"The challenge will be to ensure that payments for maintaining forests actually reach local people, and do not end up in the wrong pockets," said Frances Seymour, Director General of the Center for International Forestry Research (CIFOR) based in Indonesia.

"For the system to be effective, we will need new mechanisms for allocating payments that are efficient as well as fair," Seymour said.

A United Nations' Carbon Offset Deforestation Project Can Help Prevent Deforestation

Jan Fehse

Jan Fehse is principal consultant at EcoSecurities Global Consulting Services, which specializes in greenhouse gas emission reduction projects.

With the world's attention focused on climate change, the main question is how can global carbon emissions be reduced effectively? There is no single solution, which is why we must look seriously again at the importance of forests, in particular at an approach known as Reducing Emissions from tropical Deforestation and Degradation (REDD), and the incentives needed to achieve it.

Time to Get Serious

Policymakers have been actively debating this issue since 2005, while conservation NGOs [nongovernmental organization] have been attempting to get things off the ground for the last 15 years, only to see their hopes dashed with the exclusion of avoided deforestation from the Clean Development Mechanism (CDM) in 2001. Yet, forests are vital for managing global warming: they absorb carbon dioxide and so can counter emissions, while conversely, deforestation releases carbon dioxide into the atmosphere. Avoiding deforestation means points scored in fighting climate change.

It is now imperative that the global community finally get serious about a sector that contributes up to 25% of annual global emissions, but that has so far effectively been kept outside climate change policy. Instead it has been demonised for distracting attention away from reducing the burning of fossil fuels. This grave mistake has caused billions of tonnes of emissions to go unchallenged since 2001. Climate change is a threat of such magnitude that no options to fight it should be disregarded, especially not ones of such significance. Furthermore, deforestation also causes the loss to mankind of many other useful goods and services, such as biodiversity, soil conservation and hydrological regulation.

Deforestation also causes the loss to mankind of many other useful goods and services, such as biodiversity, soil conservation and hydrological regulation.

The timing is right because parties to the Kyoto Protocol [an international treaty to cut greenhouse gas emissions] are preparing for the next round of negotiations on emission reduction targets after 2012. REDD is seen as an attractive mechanism to entice developing countries to join more fully in the fight against climate change. In addition, the final reduction targets to be agreed upon in, hopefully, December 2009, will no doubt be influenced by the possibility of being able to use what are generally regarded as cost-effective carbon emission offsets from avoided deforestation. In other words, firmly embedding REDD into a post-2012 policy agreement is likely to make countries more comfortable to take on higher targets.

This should in itself assuage opponents who fear "market flooding", as an added supply of large amounts of REDD credits risks reducing prices and diminishing the environmental effectiveness of this market-based instrument in other sectors. These fears are unjustified when the potential increase in supply of credits is matched by a corresponding increase in demand, which are after all to be determined by the targets set in 2009. In effect this means that if OECD [Organisation for Economic Co-operation and Development, made up of 30 countries committed to democracy and a market economy] countries want to maintain the carbon incentives for non-forestry sectors and include REDD in the system, it is essential that they agree to accordingly higher targets for emissions reductions.

REDD is seen as an attractive mechanism to entice developing countries to join more fully in the fight against climate change.

Many issues need to be sorted out between now and 2009. There are technical issues such as determining baselines and setting up monitoring systems, but in principle these are manageable with the current technology and approaches already developed by forestry projects in the last decade. Data gaps should be filled rapidly once the system is up and running.

How Will REDD Work?

However, a big question remains: how will REDD actually work? Proposals range from rewarding entire countries for their national performance against a national deforestation baseline, to a CDM-like [referring to Clean Development Mechanism, a type of carbon trading already authorized by the Kyoto Treaty] crediting mechanism based on individual projects. The national approach, which seems to be favoured by most policymakers, was brought forward to capture any possible leakage from activities in a national monitoring system, such as the displacement of logging from one area to another area in the country. If most tropical countries sign up to a REDD agreement, even international leakage could be monitored and accounted for.

A further argument used in favour of a country-level reward system is that it would provide incentive for governments to use some of their powerful command-and-control and fiscal instruments to reduce deforestation. However, in reality, constraints in capacity, governance and efficiency mean the instruments available to most developing countries' governments might not be effective enough to reach the hoped-for results.

This is where project-based crediting would help. Most conservation work is achieved by grassroots activities, with people working locally alongside the agents of deforestation. Direct rewarding of their activities in a project-based crediting mechanism would seem more efficient in terms of ensuring that the incentives really benefit those who currently wield the chainsaws.

Important in this context is that credits in either case (national or project) would only be rewarded after the conservation activity has successfully been implemented. Consequently, the success of the incentive system depends on trusting the reward will indeed follow, and that it will be delivered over time periods needed to sustainably finance REDD activities. Clearly, this trust is essential for upfront investments and forward sales of carbon credits, and more conservation activities will take place if their reward does not depend upon a national government, especially one with a low credit rating, but directly on an internationally regulated, project-based system. This is key if, in addition to conservation organisations, we are serious about encouraging the private sector to engage fully in REDD activities.

The financing and facilitating power of the private sector should not be underestimated. Banks and carbon traders have embraced the CDM market and invested billions of dollars into emissions reduction projects. They also provide a credit transaction platform for projects and buyers whose core business is not carbon trading.

Kyoto compliance buyers have shown little interest in understanding the technical details of projects, which means they cannot properly assess risks associated with the forward buying of credits. Private sector intermediaries, such as this author's company, do have this expertise, and by aggregating credits from many projects in different sectors and regions, can mitigate these risks for buyers.

The private sector clearly plays an enabling role in bringing the carbon finance incentive to emissions-reducing activities, and in its search for profit it can achieve this very effectively. Similarly, if the forthcoming REDD system were to incorporate a CDM-like market-based trading system, financiers and trading intermediaries could lift REDD activities to a much larger scale than, say, the proposed fund-based alternative could ever achieve.

In short, there are good arguments for both a country-level and a project-level crediting system, yet each on their own face shortcomings. But there is no reason why they cannot be combined to reinforce each other. A registry system would be needed to avoid double-counting of avoided deforestation achievements by projects and governments. Projects could pay a commission to governments for monitoring services, so making it more attractive for governments to allow credits to be sold by others than themselves. Such a hybrid system would combine the best of both worlds and maximise much-needed reductions in tropical deforestation.

Carbon Trading Cannot Solve Amazon Rainforest Deforestation

Emily Boyd

Emily Boyd is a writer for Science Development Network— SciDev.Net—a Web site run by a nonprofit organization dedicated to providing reliable and authoritative information about science and technology for the developing world.

Some say that emissions trading under the Kyoto Protocol [an international treaty to cut greenhouse gas emissions] should be used to preserve intact areas of the Amazon rainforest as well as to restore deforested regions. This is a commendable aim—but there are several reasons why it is unlikely to work in practice.

Deforestation and the CDM System

The Clean Development Mechanism (CDM) is a key function of the Kyoto Protocol and is already being used in the emissions trading markets. It allows companies in developed countries to invest in certain projects in developing countries in return for emissions credits. For a project to be eligible for CDM credits, it must result in a net reduction of greenhouse-gas emissions. Carbon capture projects, including reforestation, do qualify for CDM credits, but conservation projects that would avoid trees being cut down in the first place do not.

Some people say that projects that avoid deforestation should be eligible for CDM credits. They say that preventing deforestation would halt a root cause of carbon dioxide being released into the atmosphere. The conversion of forests to

Emily Boyd, "Emissions Trading Cannot Solve Amazon Deforestation," *Science Development Network*, November 25, 2005. www.scidev.net. Reproduced by permission.

poorly managed agricultural land leads not only to the release of carbon from trees, but also from soils that subsequently erode away.

Including projects that avoid deforestation in the CDM [carbon] trading is unlikely to work in Brazil.

Problems with CDM Trading in Brazil Rainforests

The problem is of particular concern in Brazil, where most of the Amazon rainforest lies. Data from the Instituto de Pesquisa Ambiental da Amazônia, a research institute in northern Brazil, suggest that deforestation is responsible for emissions of an estimated 200 million tonnes of carbon each year. That is equivalent to two-thirds of Brazil's emissions of greenhouse gases and about 2.5 per cent of global carbon emissions.

But including projects that avoid deforestation in the CDM trading is unlikely to work in Brazil. Here are five reasons why.

Farmers would be likely to continue their unsustainable agricultural practices by simply moving to unprotected areas. Leaving-dioxide emissions unchanged.

First, the problem of deforestation in Brazil is tightly linked to internal migration. If an area were declared protected by a CDM project, farmers would be likely to continue their unsustainable agricultural practices by simply moving to unprotected areas. Leaving-dioxide emissions unchanged.

To avoid this, alternative economic opportunities would have to be offered to the farmers or effective sanctions would need to be applied. Controlling deforestation and the emissions that result from it would mean controlling migration.

But this is difficult to do, say the authorities, because local institutions have limited funds and staff.

Second, political disagreement on this issue between different groups in the country which has prevented Brazil from taking a united position in international negotiations. The Brazilian government opposes the inclusion within the CDM of projects that avoid deforestation, arguing that farmers would simply migrate to non-protected areas and cut down the trees there. Some non-governmental organisations and government officials do support the inclusion of 'avoided deforestation' projects in the CDM to obtain much-needed funds for conservation efforts.

Third, 'perverse incentives' encourage deforestation in Brazil. It is cheaper to clear new land areas for the international beef and soya bean markets than to invest in already deforested regions. As long as the prices for agricultural commodities such as soya and biofuel exports remain high, illegal agricultural settlements will continue to use resources unsustainably. The reason for this is that soya is established on grasslands pushing cattle pastures further into forested areas.

The way forward for Brazil may be to focus on the existing system of fiscal measures to encourage forest conservation.

Fourth, influencing the activities of small-scale farmers will have little impact on the deforestation problem. Some suggest that financing supplied through carbon credits might provide such farmers with much-needed incentives to switch to sustainable methods. However, small farms in Brazil only account for about 20 per cent of deforestation and larger farms are unlikely to adopt sustainable methods, such as no-tillage agriculture and agroforestry. So the use of such technologies will only be a marginal solution to the deforestation problem.

Finally, under the Kyoto Protocol, only one per cent of all CDM projects can relate to land use and forestry. It is also unlikely that the issue of deforestation will be resolved in climate negotiations as long as forums created to resolve the problem, such as the UN Forum on Forests, are unable to reach agreement.

Instead of debating whether or not the CDM should include conservation, the way forward for Brazil may be to focus on the existing system of fiscal measures to encourage forest conservation. This system has reportedly made significant progress in several states, including Minas Gerais. Another useful action would be to prevent perverse incentives, for example by using certification standards to ensure that soya beans are not grown on newly cleared lands or lands adjacent to forests. Such national policy measures could very well provide more tangible results than can be achieved under the international carbon market.

Carbon Trading May Put Mature Tropical Forests at Risk

Science Daily

Science Daily *is one of the Internet's leading online magazines and Web portals devoted to science, technology, and medicine. The following viewpoint is adapted from materials provided by Conservation International.*

In an ironic twist, 11 countries that have avoided widespread destruction of their tropical forest are at risk of being left out of an emerging carbon market intended to promote rainforest conservation to combat climate change.

A study published August 14 [2007] in the *Public Library of Science Biology* journal warns that the "high forest cover with low rates of deforestation" (HFLD) nations could become the most vulnerable targets for deforestation if the Kyoto Protocol [an international treaty to cut greenhouse gas emissions] and upcoming negotiations on carbon trading fail to include intact standing forest.

The study by scientists from Conservation International (CI), the South African National Biodiversity Institute, and the University of California-Santa Barbara calls for the HFLD countries to receive "preventive credits" under any carbon trading mechanism to provide incentive for them to protect their intact tropical forest. Otherwise, the same market and economic forces that cause deforestation elsewhere will quickly descend on regions that so far have avoided significant loss, the authors say.

Cutting and burning tropical forests releases the atmospheric carbon they store, contributing significantly to global

Conservation International, "Carbon Trading Proposal May Put Mature Tropical Forests at Risk, Scientists Warn," *ScienceDaily.com*, August 14, 2007. Reproduced by permission.

climate change. The HFLD countries contain 20 percent of Earth's remaining tropical forest, including some of the richest ecosystems.

"Given the very large—and likely still underestimated—role of tropical deforestation in causing climate change, these forest-rich countries should be at the forefront of worldwide efforts to sequester carbon, rather than being left out entirely," said CI President Russell A. Mittermeier, an author of the study. "With this paper, we hope to highlight this critical issue and put it on the table for future negotiations."

New rules being discussed by the [international community] . . . are likely to create a carbon market for countries that reduce their deforestation.

Excluding Existing Rainforests

Until now, the Kyoto Protocol and subsequent discussions have focused on carbon credits for new or replanted forests that replace the carbon storage services of destroyed forests. New rules being discussed by the U.N. [United Nations] Framework Convention on Climate Change for implementation subsequent to Kyoto are likely to create a carbon market for countries that reduce their deforestation from levels of recent years.

That would cover countries that have lost large portions of their original tropical forest, as well as those that still have more than half their forest cover but face current high rates of deforestation. In contrast, 11 HFLD countries with more than half their original forest intact and low rates of current deforestation would receive no credits for standing forests.

"The minute that you exclude those countries, their forests lose economic value in the global carbon market, leaving governments with little reason to protect them," said study co-author Gustavo Fonseca of CI and Brazil's Universidade Federal de Minas Gerais.

---

11 ... countries with more than half their original forest intact and low rates of current deforestation would receive no credits for standing forests [under the new rules].

The HFLD countries are Panama, Colombia, Democratic Republic of Congo, Peru, Belize, Gabon, Guyana, Suriname, Bhutan and Zambia, along with French Guiana, which is a French territory. Three of them—Guyana, Suriname and French Guiana—comprise much of the Guayana Shield region of the northern Amazon that is the largest intact tract of tropical forest on Earth. In addition, portions of other large non-HFLD countries are in the same situation. For example, although Brazil has four other major ecosystems, the Brazilian Amazon faces a similar circumstance as HFLD countries.

According to the study, preventive credits for HFLD countries at a conservative carbon price of U.S. $10 per ton would be worth hundreds of millions of dollars a year, providing governments with significant economic incentive to protect tropical forests that store atmospheric carbon and supply essential natural benefits for local populations such as clean water, food, medicines and natural resources.

CI believes any carbon credit mechanism should include full representation, participation and consultation by indigenous and local communities of tropical forest regions to ensure that conservation and development programs proceed in accordance with their rights and traditional ways of life as stewards of the crucial ecosystems in which they live.

Along with Fonseca and Mittermeier, the study's other authors are Carlos Manuel Rodriguez and Lee Hannah of CI, Guy Midgley of the Kirstenbosch Research Center at the South African National Biodiversity Institute, and Jonah Busch of the Donald Bren School of Environmental Science and Management at UC [University of California]-Santa Barbara.

Carbon Trading Projects for Reducing Emissions from Deforestation Could Hurt Indigenous Peoples

Angeli Mehta and Jutta Kill

Angeli Mehta and Jutta Kill are forest and climate change campaigners for FERN, a European organization that coordinates efforts to save the world's forests and support the struggles of forest peoples.

Urgent action is needed to slow forest loss, not least because forests are major storehouses of carbon. However, it is crucial to understand that the value of forests goes beyond their carbon storage properties, especially for forest peoples. The outcome of the climate talks will impact on who manages forests and what is allowed to happen on forest lands, with enormous implications for the livelihoods and welfare of the hundreds of millions of forest peoples in tropical and subtropical countries. Their future will be shaped by how the rest of the world raises the money and designs and implements plans to prevent further forest loss. If failures of past efforts to address deforestation are not to be repeated, principles of respect for human rights and the land and customary rights of indigenous peoples must become a central element of agreements aimed at reducing emissions from deforestation. To date they have been, at worst, absent from the debate and at best, an afterthought.

How to Prevent Deforestation

Urgent action is needed to preserve the globe's last remaining forests. It's now recognised that deforestation—especially in

Angeli Mehta and Jutta Kill, "Briefing: Seeing 'RED'?: 'Avoided Deforestation' and the Rights of Indigenous Peoples and Local Communities," *FERN.org*, November 2007. Reproduced by permission.

149

the tropics—is a major contributor to global CO_2 [carbon dioxide] emissions, and needs to be tackled. The thorny question is how?

Support is growing apace for reducing emissions from deforestation—whereby countries are paid to prevent or slow forest loss which would otherwise have occurred. It's an attractive idea because it could provide a relatively low cost mechanism to help fight climate change, whilst—potentially—improving living standards for some of the world's poorest people. It would also protect the rich biodiversity of the globe's original forests. But as ever, the devil is in the detail.

It is crucial to understand that the value of forests goes beyond their carbon storage properties, especially for forest peoples.

The Bali climate conference in December 2007 [discussed] ... proposals for economic incentives to encourage tropical countries to protect carbon reservoirs in their forests and [delegates agreed to include such ideas in future discussions for a post-2012 climate agreement]....

However, the world need not wait until 2012 to begin this vital work. It's true that the rules for the first commitment period of the Kyoto Protocol [an international treaty designed to cut greenhouse gas emissions] are set and don't include any provision to link so-called 'reduced emissions' from deforestation with carbon markets, but action could begin now if other funding mechanisms are used.

Who Benefits?

Governments and global agencies are talking in detail about how to fund reductions in emissions from (tropical) forest loss. 'RED' will be a much-used acronym at [future] ... UN [United Nations] climate conference[s].... It stands for 'reducing emissions from deforestation', or for 'reducing emissions from deforestation and forest degradation' in the case of REDD.

The main thrust of the proposals on the table, both from governments and international conservation organisations, is for Northern industrialised nations to pay [less developed] Southern countries to reduce forest clearance within their borders.

They claim that powerful economic incentives are needed to counter the economic drivers of deforestation (e.g. conversion to agriculture or for agro-fuel plantations). Countries that demonstrate verifiable reductions in deforestation, or maintenance of forest cover, would be paid compensation through a global and/or regional fund or would be allowed to sell carbon credits that permit additional emissions elsewhere.

There is no rigorous discussion of how to avoid the social risks associated with carbon forest projects.

Their proposals claim that policies to reduce emissions from deforestation will bring increased income for some of the world's poorest—but how is this to come about?

There's no clarity here because there is no rigorous discussion of how to avoid the social risks associated with carbon forest projects, which have already seen indigenous peoples and local communities impoverished by abusive and costly forest protection contracts and evicted from their lands. For instance: Who will have the right to negotiate? How can corruption be prevented in what will be lucrative enterprises? How will indigenous peoples and local communities be guaranteed the rewards for protecting forests? How will evictions be prevented and forest peoples' customary rights and access to forests upheld? Who will absorb unforeseen costs? What happens if the carbon is released unexpectedly, for example through forest fire? These questions need to be answered before governments start negotiating a post-2012 agreement that includes forests.

There is also little clarity about which activities and which actors might receive funds or rewards through measures to reduce emissions from deforestation. Many NGOs [nongovernmental organizations] are concerned that industrial logging operations claiming to reduce forest degradation, if extra carbon funding were available, may be rewarded to continue unsustainable logging practices.

Evidence from India, Brazil and Ecuador shows how indigenous peoples often don't get the levels of income and employment promised.

Sir Nicholas Stern, who led the UK [United Kingdom] Government's review of climate change, believes that the key to effective forest management is "establishing and enforcing clear property rights to forest lands and determining the rights and responsibilities of the communities, landowners and loggers." This, he says, should involve local communities and 'take account of their interests and structures'.

The World Agro-Forestry Centre claims that environmental payments schemes can work if proper attention is given to rights and equity issues. They cite their programme operating in Indonesia, Nepal and the Philippines called Rewarding Upland Poor for Environmental Services (Rupes). One positive example they point to in Sumberjaya, western Indonesia—where forced evictions were the norm ten years ago—the government has awarded conditional land tenure to more than 6,000 farmers—which has doubled local land value, reduced corruption and increased farmers' incomes.

But more often than not, they don't. Forest protection schemes involving carbon trading that have failed to properly address governance and livelihood concerns have not fared so well. Evidence from India, Brazil and Ecuador shows how indigenous peoples often don't get the levels of income and employment promised.

Proving clear title to the land is a huge problem for many of the world's poorest ... so inevitably some schemes have generated conflict.

Proving clear title to the land is a huge problem for many of the world's poorest and the customary land and resource rights of indigenous peoples are often not recognised by national laws—so inevitably some schemes have generated conflict, and inequalities between peoples have got worse.

In the Noel Kempff National Park in Bolivia—where a consortium bought out logging concession owners in order to extend the park—the costs of forest protection fell disproportionately on the local populations. People faced restrictions on hunting, fishing, etc.; public roads deteriorated after the termination of the logging concessions, so transport costs for local communities increased.

Some advocates of avoided deforestation programmes point out that there are emerging certification standards which provide safeguards for new avoided deforestation schemes. However, it has become clear that often those voluntary 'standards' simply are not enforced. Take the example of the logging and tree plantation sectors. The Forest Stewardship Council's standards, which are supposed to respect indigenous land tenure and uphold the principle of free, prior and informed consent, have been found lacking in some countries, including several that are now the focus of the 'Avoided Deforestation' debate. It's worth pointing out that the Ecuadorian pine plantations project—for all its problems—won FSC [Forest Stewardship Council] certification.

Funding: The How?

The Brazilian government has proposed that there should be an international fund to compensate efforts to reduce emissions from deforestation. Sir Nicholas Stern suggests such an approach could provide for the setting up of targeted pilot schemes—to get practical experience. This may be a good idea—depending on how the public funds are administered.

The World Bank [an international organization that provides development assistance to developing nations] is putting avoided deforestation at the forefront of its proposals for a new Global Forest Partnership. The Forest Carbon Partnership Facility, which the Bank . . . [launched] at the UN conference in Bali in December 2007, links this 'mega-fund' for forests to carbon trading. World Bank documents describing this carbon partnership facility define in great detail the rights of buyers and sellers yet remain surprisingly vague on what exactly is being bought and sold. Essentially, Southern countries would, in compensation for reducing deforestation, sell the carbon locked up in their forests. But whether these payments will allow the Northern industrialised nations or corporate buyers of forest carbon to continue polluting as usual in return for their purchase the World Bank, documents do not reveal.

The uncomfortable fact is that, so far, carbon trading schemes . . . haven't reduced greenhouse gas emissions [or] . . . provided sustainable development benefits.

A group of originally eight countries, called the Coalition of Rainforest Nations, and many conservation NGOs believe a scheme based on the carbon market is the only way to raise the amount of money that would be needed for sufficiently attractive levels of compensation.

We disagree. The uncomfortable fact is that, so far, carbon trading schemes (like the Kyoto Protocol's Clean Development Mechanism) haven't reduced greenhouse gas emissions, nor have they provided sustainable development benefits to communities in the Southern nations selling the credits.

Carbon trading schemes also allow 'business as usual' for Northern polluters with continued reliance on fossil fuels, and provide no encouragement to change patterns of conspicuous consumption.

Moreover, it's impossible to verify how much carbon is actually being saved—if any. The principle of the Kyoto Protocol's Clean Development Mechanism is that carbon credits should fund projects that would not otherwise have gone ahead—in many cases this has proved to be nonsense.

Worryingly, the momentum for a carbon-trading approach is shifting the debate away from how to promote a just transition from dependence on fossil fuels through public investment, regulation, shifting of subsidies, and taxation.

Some critics of the World Bank's Carbon Partnership Facility proposal believe that the Bank is trying to harness avoided deforestation funds to finance its controversial Forest Strategy, a review of which is imminent and said to reveal major shortcomings of the Bank's implementation of this strategy.

[RED proposals] will have ... enormous implications for the livelihoods and welfare of the hundreds of millions of forest peoples in tropical and sub-tropical countries.

Certainly in its many negotiations with Southern country governments, the World Bank has so far failed to engage forest peoples and local communities and its latest proposals to create a Forest Carbon Partnership Facility have seemingly had little, and only last minute, input even from Southern governments, which doesn't augur well for their success.

What's being discussed and negotiated now will have an impact on who manages forests and what is allowed to happen on forest land, with enormous implications for the livelihoods and welfare of the hundreds of millions of forest peoples in tropical and sub-tropical countries.

It is ... essential that any agreement aimed at reducing the emissions from deforestation ... [must respect the] human and customary rights of forest peoples.

Their future will be shaped by how the rest of the world raises the money and designs and implements plans to prevent further forest loss.

It is therefore essential that any agreement aimed at reducing the emissions from deforestation in the context of the climate negotiations must adhere to the principles of respect for human and customary rights of forest peoples. Land rights, customary rights and the free, prior and informed consent of forest peoples who live in, and depend on, the world's forests will have to become central issues in the debate.

One crucial lesson from the many failed initiatives to slow deforestation is that forest peoples and local communities must be fully involved in the debate from the beginning. Sadly, that lesson has yet to be learned by those tabling proposals and launching carbon partnership facilities to reduce emission from deforestation at the Bali climate conference.

CHAPTER 4

How Should the Voluntary Carbon Offset Market Be Regulated?

Chapter Preface

One of the most debated issues concerning carbon offset projects is how they should be regulated to ensure that they effectively reduce global greenhouse gas emissions. At the international level, the United Nations has set up mechanisms for approving carbon offset projects already under its mandatory emissions reduction system. The Kyoto Protocol, for example, permits a variety of emissions reduction projects in its Clean Development Mechanism (CDM) program—including energy efficiency, fuel switching, forestation, transportation, and renewable energy technologies such as wind, solar, hydro, geothermal, and waste biogas—but requires that such projects be certified to ensure that they produce the expected amount of emissions reduction.

The CDM certification process has several steps. First, a Kyoto signatory country that wants to fund a carbon offset project in a developing country must win the approval of the host country. An application must be filed with the Designated National Authority (DNA), an agency set up in the developing country to work with the Kyoto program. The DNA reviews the project to check whether it complies with national sustainable development criteria and local environmental requirements.

If the project passes the DNA stage, it is then referred to the Designated Operational Entities (DOE), a third party verification company accredited by the United Nations. The submittal to the DOE is called the Project Design Document (PDD), which uses a specific format developed by the CDM Executive Board, an entity that supervises the CDM program under the terms of the Kyoto treaty. The PDD must include a detailed description of the project and the expected greenhouse gas emission reductions, and generally explain how the project will produce and measure concrete, long-term emissions reductions. The DOE reviews the project, and if it is approved, registers it, allowing the project to be implemented and to begin generating emissions reduction credits.

Once the project is operational, the DOE must verify all claimed emissions reductions to authorize the issuance of Certified Emission Reductions (CERs), commonly known as carbon credits or offsets. Each of these credits is equal to a reduction of one ton of carbon dioxide or its equivalent. DOE verifies and certifies emissions reductions on an annual or biennial basis. Once the emissions reductions are verified and certified, CERs are issued by the CDM Executive Board.

One of the biggest concerns in the certification process is the issue of so-called additionality—that is, whether the project would have happened anyway, even if carbon credits were not awarded. If the project would have been built even without the CDM program, then it would not really reduce emissions more than if the CERs were not granted. To ensure that a project is additional, therefore, the CDM board has developed rules that must be used for evaluating the additionality of each carbon offset project. Currently, the CDM Executive Board deems a project additional if its supporters can show that realistic alternative scenarios to the proposed project would be more economically attractive or that the project faces financial barriers without the help of the CDM program.

Concerns about the standards used to evaluate CDM projects have been somewhat allayed by the development of an independent tool called the Gold Standard. The Gold Standard was created in 2003 by three nongovernmental organizations—the World Wide Fund for Nature (WWF), SouthSouth-North, and Helio International—and has been since endorsed by more than fifty environmental and development organizations. In addition to requiring projects to comply with the rules set forth by the CDM Executive Board, the Gold Standard imposes various other requirements on CDM projects to hold them to the highest possible standards for quality and effectiveness. Notably, Gold Standard projects are limited to renewable energy and energy efficiency technologies, and cannot include carbon sequestration projects such as tree plantings. The Gold Standard methodology is used by DOEs for CDM projects but also can be applied to Joint Implementation (JI) projects, another type of carbon offset program authorized under the Kyoto treaty. In 2006, a Voluntary Gold Standard was developed for evaluating carbon offset projects in the voluntary carbon markets as well.

As of July 2008, 1,128 projects have been registered as CDM projects, and if these projects succeed, they may reduce global greenhouse gas emissions by an estimated 220 million tons of carbon dioxide (or its equivalent) each year. Critics have complained that, due to the complexities involved in approving and certifying projects, the CDM program has a low rate of project approval, resulting in little impact on overall greenhouse gas emissions. Yet at the same time, careful scrutiny is necessary to ensure that projects succeed in reducing emissions.

Many experts have called for similar regulation of the voluntary carbon offset markets, including the U.S. market. In the United States, a variety of private organizations have been created to sell carbon offsets to companies and individuals, and although some of these organizations claim to use a voluntary Gold Standard to evaluate their offset projects, the government has not yet created any type of regulatory structure to provide oversight of these activities. The viewpoints in this chapter explore the question of how these voluntary carbon offset markets should be regulated.

The Problem with Individual Carbon Offsets Now Is That They Are Not Properly Regulated

Moises Velasquez-Manoff

Moises Velasquez-Manoff is a correspondent for the Christian Science Monitor, *an international daily newspaper published by the First Church of Christ, Scientist in Boston, Massachusetts.*

In 2006, "carbon neutral" became the New Oxford American Dictionary's word of the year, evidence not only of the "greening" of our culture, but of our language as well. As scientists predict another bout of record-setting temperatures this year, climate concerns may soon "green" our wallets as well. By all accounts, 2007 is poised to see the industry of carbon neutrality—so-called carbon offsetting—grow dramatically.

A Lack of Standards

In theory, the idea is simple. The consumer pays a third party to remove a quantity of carbon (in the form of a greenhouse gas) equal to what he or she emits. But how voluntary carbon offsets actually work is unclear at best, and potentially fraudulent at worst, say experts.

The problem: No current certification or monitoring system has any teeth, and there is no easy way to confirm that offsetting companies are doing what they promise. Now, various organizations are scrambling to provide standards for what experts call a fragmented market with a product of drastically varying quality.

Moises Velasquez-Manoff, "Do Carbon Offsets Live Up to Their Promise?" *Christian Science Monitor*, January 10, 2007. Reproduced by permission from *Christian Science Monitor*. www.csmonitor.com.

The first-ever ranking of carbon offsetters recently released by Clean Air-Cool Planet, a nonprofit in Portsmouth, N.H., graded 30 companies on a scale of 1 to 10; tellingly, three-quarters scored below 5. Critics, meanwhile, question whether the carbon market might be a dangerous distraction at a time when decisive action is needed to avert climate catastrophe.

"On the one hand, there is the potential benefit of educating people through offsets," says Dan Becker, director of Sierra Club's [an environmental group] global warming program. "On the other hand, if people view offsets like papal indulgences that allow you to continue to pollute, then it's probably not a good idea."

No current certification or monitoring system has any teeth, and there is no easy way to confirm that offsetting companies are doing what they promise.

A Group Market

Many companies have nonetheless moved to make carbon neutrality part of their 21st-century brand identity. Travelocity and Expedia now offer customers the option of offsetting carbon emissions associated with their trips for a few extra dollars. In 2005, "Syriana" became the first carbon-neutral movie. In 2006, "An Inconvenient Truth" followed suit to become the first such documentary. With the purchase of 170,000 tons of carbon offsets, HSBC declared itself the first-ever carbon-neutral bank. Other companies, including Google and Ben & Jerry's—not to mention musical groups such as the Dave Matthews Band—are moving toward, or have arrived at, various levels of carbon neutrality.

And that's just the beginning, say analysts. The volume of metric tons of carbon traded on the voluntary market doubled last year over 2005. It's widely expected to double again in 2007. Of 92 companies polled by The Conference Board, a nonprofit business research organization, three-quarters were actively computing their carbon footprint. While only 15 percent were currently trading on the voluntary carbon market, 40 percent were considering it. Carbon was the topic du jour in more than two-thirds of the corporate boardrooms polled.

Existing Carbon Markets

Carbon markets fall into two broad categories:

- *The cap-and-trade system.* Countries that have ratified the Kyoto Protocol, an amendment to the global treaty on climate change, participate in this system by setting a limit, or cap, on greenhouse-gas emissions. Those companies that emit less than their allotment receive credits that they can sell on carbon exchanges. Those that emit more must purchase credits in order to avoid financial penalties. (The voluntary Chicago Climate Exchange also operates this way.) Proponents of this system trust the innovative power of the free market to promote energy efficiency.

- *The voluntary carbon market.* In the United States, the market for carbon offsets is voluntary, driven primarily by corporations seeking to enhance their brand identity or to familiarize themselves with what they consider to be an inevitability.

Many offsets sold on this market are what Ricardo Bayon, director of Ecosystem Marketplace, a San Francisco-based information provider on ecosystems services, calls "gourmet." Their value lies not in the compliance, but in the prestige of achieving carbon neutrality. At first glance, this type of offset appears more straightforward: A consumer pays for a carbon-removal service.

Dig a little deeper, however, and it gets more complicated. There are many ways to remove carbon from the air, each operating on a different time scale and all of them of different "quality." You can capture greenhouse gases by planting trees. You can also prevent greenhouse gas from entering the atmosphere by burning methane released from animal manure and landfills. (As a greenhouse gas, methane is 23 times more potent than CO_2 [carbon dioxide].) Or you can preempt its release by building alternative-energy sources such as wind- and solar-power devices.

Unless you're willing to visit Uganda in 20 years to verify the existence of a new tree, a carbon offset is arguably invisible.

Compounding an offset's inscrutability is its intangibility. Unless you're willing to visit Uganda in 20 years to verify the existence of a new tree, a carbon offset is arguably invisible. "The carbon market is particularly difficult because of that issue," says Mark Trexler, president of Trexler Climate + Energy Services in Portland, Ore., the firm commissioned to author Clean Air-Cool Planet's (CA-CP) guide to carbon offsets. "You're dealing with stuff in the future in many cases that hasn't happened yet."

The Guide to Carbon Offsets

CA-CP's "A Consumer's Guide to Retail Carbon Offset Providers" attempts to wrangle a semblance of order from what one industry insider calls the "Wild West." It ranks offsetting companies on factors like transparency, third-party certification, their efforts to educate consumers, and how well they prove they're not selling the same carbon offset more than once.

CA-CP's ranking effort is the first in what's likely to be a burgeoning industry effort at standardization. Two San Francisco organizations, Business for Social Responsibility and Ecosystem Marketplace, recently joined forces to write guides on the voluntary carbon market, and Ecosystem Marketplace is about to release a book on the topic. This spring, the Center for Resource Solutions in San Francisco plans to release a certification standard it hopes will be universally adopted.

Additionality is determined by answering a deceptively simple question: Would a project have happened anyway?

Central to the CA-CP report—and to the debate on how to gauge an offset's quality—is the topic of "additionality." Additionality is determined by answering a deceptively simple question: Would a project have happened anyway? If yes, the offset cannot be said to have additionality. If no, then it qualifies as a true offset. Simple—except that no one agrees on what *could* have happened.

"You put a bunch of climate wonks in a room, it's the one [topic] they're going to talk about most," says Mr. Bayon. "And it's the one that has bedeviled every single climate discussion I've ever seen."

But while experts disagree on the effectiveness of the carbon market at averting global warming, nearly everyone agrees on two points. First, the fact that people are beginning to factor in the cost of their carbon footprint when doing business is good. "You're starting to put a price on the emissions of carbon," says Bayon. "That cost begins to filter into your operations. And you start saying to yourself, 'Should I throw that 10 or 20 bucks out of the window?'"

Second, the more money invested in renewable energy, the better. "That has an important effect in the aggregate," says Bogdan Vasi, assistant professor at Columbia's School of International and Public Affairs in New York City. "As more and more people make these choices, they are creating a market, and slowly it's shifting the proportion of renewable energy to fossil-fuel energy."

But ultimately the carbon-offset market is more a phase than a destination, says Jonathan Isham, professor of international environmental economics at Middlebury College in Vermont. "We really want a world where, in a generation, we don't need offsets anymore," he says. "Once we get the legislation we need, prices will reflect the social costs of carbon."

The fact that people are beginning to factor in the cost of their carbon footprint when doing business is good.

More Trees Not Necessarily the Way to a Cooler Earth

Everybody loves trees. They're beautiful, big, and green. Unfortunately, planting them may not be the best approach to reduce global warming, say scientists. While a tree does suck up carbon, its net cooling effect depends on latitude, according to a collaborative study from Lawrence Livermore National Laboratory in Livermore, Calif. Only trees planted at tropical latitudes have a net cooling effect. Those at temperate latitudes actually warm the planet.

And unless a forest is permanent (and who can guarantee that?), trees only temporarily sequester atmospheric carbon. When they burn or decompose, the carbon they contain is released back into the atmosphere. In tropical countries, where trees are most effective as a cooling agent, they're often up against poverty and political instability. "Does some guy wake up and say, 'Now I'm the dictator of the country. I want a golf course?'" says Michael Dorsey, a professor of environmental studies at Dartmouth College in Hanover, N.H. "There's the big issue."

Still, a tree's value shouldn't be discounted. While not the ideal carbon solution, they do increase biodiversity and decrease soil erosion. Most important, their natural appeal makes them ready-made symbols. "We do support tree-planting projects to get our employees engaged," says Erin Meezan, director of environmental affairs at Interface Inc., a textile company with an environmental bent. "It's one of the easiest things for people to understand. If you start getting into anaerobic digesters and underground injection, we lose them."

The U.S. Government Should Provide Guidelines and Oversight of the Domestic Carbon Offset Market

Derik Broekhoff

Derik Broekhoff is a senior associate at the World Resources Institute, an environmental think-tank based in Washington, D.C.

Carbon offsets are an innovative tool for allowing companies and individuals to reduce greenhouse gas emissions beyond what they can easily achieve on their own. In the past two years, interest in carbon offsets has grown dramatically as companies and concerned consumers have sought ways to help mitigate climate change. However, the global market for voluntary carbon offsets is currently unregulated, which has led to growing concerns about whether buyers are really getting what they are paying for....

Why Are Some People Concerned About the Voluntary Carbon Offset Market?

Voluntary carbon offsets have been traded in relatively small volumes and on a demonstration basis since the late 1980s. Some organizations, such as the Climate Trust in Oregon, have many years of experience in purchasing and retiring offsets on behalf of clients or customers (the Climate Trust was established in 1997 to assist new power plants in Oregon to meet a state regulatory requirement for net CO_2 [carbon dioxide] emissions).... [However], there has been a dramatic increase in the last two years in the number of voluntary offset transactions, with an accompanying expansion in the number of suppliers. Unlike the Kyoto Protocol's CDM offset market [Clean Development Mechanism, a type of carbon offset trading created by the Kyoto Protocol, an international treaty to cut greenhouse gas emissions] however, where there are clear rules, standards, and oversight mechanisms, the voluntary market is operating in a regulatory vacuum. Many observers are concerned about the lack of standards and oversight for voluntary carbon offsets, and wonder whether buyers are truly getting what they pay for, i.e., real emission reductions.

The issue is not so much a question about the integrity of carbon offset providers. Most suppliers in the market today are well-meaning private companies and non-profit organizations that sincerely want to help their customers do good for the environment. The questions that arise are really about the definition of the "commodity" being sold. Carbon offsets are an intangible good, and as such their value and integrity depend entirely on how they are defined, represented, and guaranteed. What the market lacks are common standards for how such representations and guarantees are made and enforced.

Carbon offsets are an intangible good, and as such their value and integrity depend entirely on how they are defined, represented, and guaranteed.

What Elements Are Necessary for a Carbon Offset Standard?

Much of the literature on carbon offsets point out that credible offsets must be "real, surplus, permanent, verifiable, and enforceable"—or some variation of these terms. Different sources do not always agree on the definitions of these criteria, however, and having a "standard" for carbon offsets really depends on how they are interpreted. What the criteria boil down to are three things, all of which need some form of official certification or oversight to create a true carbon offset "commodity": (1) accounting standards; (2) monitoring and verification standards; and (3) registration and enforcement systems.

1. GHG Emission Reduction Accounting Standards

Accounting standards address the actual quantification of GHG [greenhouse gas] reductions that carbon offsets represent. Accounting standards are a first-order requirement for ensuring that a ton of emission reductions from one project is the same as a ton from another, and ensure that offsets are "real, surplus, and permanent."

The most important part of offset project accounting is . . . "additionality"—that is, whether the . . . project . . . would have happened anyway.

As might be expected, a lot of work has been done over the years to develop accounting standards for offsets. In December 2005, the World Resources Institute (WRI) and the World Business Council for Sustainable Development (WBCSD) [two private organizations] published the *Greenhouse Gas Protocol for Project Accounting* ("Project Protocol"), which provides a general framework for quantifying emission reductions from offset projects, based on the accumulated knowledge of an international group of experts from businesses, governments, and environmental groups. It has since been supplemented with two sector-specific accounting protocols, one for land use and forestry projects, the other for renewable energy and energy efficiency projects. These documents provide an internationally recognized basis for the elaboration of detailed accounting standards for specific types of projects. The largest body of standard accounting methodologies established to date exists under the Kyoto Protocol's Clean Development Mechanism. Very few of the carbon offsets sold in the voluntary market, however, explicitly follow the WRI/WBCSD Project Protocol or CDM methodologies.

Probably the most important part of offset project accounting is making a determination about "additionality"—that is, whether the purchase of emission reductions really enabled (or induced) a project to happen, or whether the purchase is essentially being wasted on a project that would have happened anyway (in which case its emission reductions effectively have zero value for the purpose of offsetting emissions). Many would say that "additionality" is the key to the environmental integrity of an offset purchase—but it is also vexingly hard to determine in many cases. It has proven very difficult to establish true standards for additionality, and even the CDM requires regulators to make essentially subjective judgments about it on a case-by-case basis. Two recent reports on the voluntary carbon offset market suggest that many providers do not clearly indicate how they determine the additionality of their projects. A standard set of guidance or criteria would aid the credibility of offset markets tremendously.

2. Monitoring and Verification Standards

Monitoring and verification standards are required to ensure that offset projects perform as expected and to quantify their actual emission reductions. Monitoring protocols are generally developed in conjunction with accounting protocols. Verification usually requires the services of a third-party professional verifier, or a government regulator. If third-party verifiers are used, they need to meet minimum qualifications and have some expertise related to the types of projects they are verifying. This is one of the biggest gaps in the voluntary carbon offset market right now. Although there is a generic international standard for the accreditation of verifiers, and there are certainly verifiers with well-established reputations for competence and integrity, a publicly accountable certification process for verifiers could greatly enhance the credibility of the voluntary offset market.

Finally, verification does not mean very much without clear accounting and monitoring standards against which to verify. This emphasizes the need to adopt common accounting and reporting standards.

One concern about the voluntary offset market as it continues to grow is the possibility that suppliers may sell the same reductions to multiple buyers.

---

3. Registration and Enforcement Systems

One concern about the voluntary offset market as it continues to grow is the possibility that suppliers may sell the same reductions to multiple buyers, because there is no central authority to track their transactions. Related to this, questions can arise in some instances about who "owns" emission reductions and who in fact has the right to sell them. In some cases, multiple parties may conceivably lay claim to the same reduction. For example, both the manufacturer and the installer of energy efficient lightbulbs might want to claim the emission reductions caused by the lightbulbs—as might the owners of the power plants where the reductions actually occur. Right now, establishing the right to an offset reduction largely consists of making public marketing claims and trying to exclude others from doing the same. . . .

A number of organizations involved in the [offset] industry have initiated efforts . . . to develop voluntary standards.

Is Anyone Trying to Create Standards for the Voluntary Carbon Offset Market?

To address the current shortcomings in the voluntary carbon offset market, a number of organizations involved in the industry have initiated efforts . . . to develop voluntary standards. The first such standards were the WRI/WBCSD Project Protocol and the ISO [International Organization for Standardization, a group that develops international standards on a variety of subjects] 14064 standard. The WRI/WBCSD Project Protocol is a set of guidance documents for offset project accounting, while the ISO 14064 standard is a checklist of essential accounting elements. Neither is a full-fledged standard for determining the emission reductions for specific technologies or practices—although both together provide a toolkit for policymakers to create such standards. Furthermore, while the ISO standard does cover verification, neither the WRI/WBCSD Project Protocol nor the ISO standards cover all three of the required elements for a fully standardized carbon offset commodity noted above.

Other standard-setting efforts have tackled different pieces of the puzzle. The California Climate Action Registry (CCAR) [an organization created by the state of California that encourages businesses and government agencies to measure and report their GHG emissions] is developing a series of accounting standards for specific types of offset projects, compatible with the WRI/WBCSD Project Protocol. So far they have approved protocols for forestry sequestration projects and agricultural methane digesters. Projects can be registered with CCAR, and CCAR maintains a list of accredited verifiers. CCAR does not yet have a facility for tracking trades or retiring offset credits, although this may be developed in the future. Similarly, the U.S. Environmental Protection Agency Climate Leaders Program has begun developing a set of standards for quantifying emission reductions for several types of projects. These standards are still in draft form, however, and would need to be supplemented with monitoring and verification standards and a registry to establish a credible carbon offset commodity.

The Center for Resource Solutions (CRS) (a non-profit environmental group) has recently completed work on a

"Green-e GHG Product Standard." Under this standard, CRS will certify carbon offsets that are created under programs that already have credible accounting and verification standards in place. The CRS standard does seek to provide an enforcement mechanism. but relies on other programs for accounting and verification rules.

[Other nongovernmental groups such as] The Climate Group (based in London), the International Emissions Trading Association, and the World Economic Forum are currently developing a global "Voluntary Carbon Standard" (VCS) that will in principle cover accounting rules, verification standards, and the establishment of a registration and enforcement system. Initially, the VCS will most likely reference CDM accounting and verification standards, although it may incorporate other standards over time. Its credibility will largely rest on the decisions of designated verifiers, which will effectively be responsible for its enforcement in place of a central regulatory authority.

The Chicago Climate Exchange (CCX) has operated a voluntary [carbon] trading system since 2003 that includes a carbon offset component. In principle CCX offsets can be used to voluntarily offset emissions for companies and individuals who are not CCX members, just as CDM offsets can. The CCX program includes proprietary accounting rules, verification standards, and a registry to track credits and project information. One of the criticisms of the CCX, however, is that little information is publicly available about its standards and individual projects.

Most of the "standards" developed under voluntary initiatives to date do not incorporate all of the elements of a true carbon offset commodity standard.

Other voluntary carbon offset standards, including the "CDM Gold Standard," primarily reference the CDM's accounting and verification requirements. They do not provide separate accreditation of verifiers, nor have they established strong registry or enforcement systems.

In short, most of the "standards" developed under voluntary initiatives to date do not incorporate all of the elements of a true carbon offset commodity standard. Some of these initiatives could develop into full-fledged standards and oversight programs, but are not there yet. The VCS may cover all the bases when it is launched, but it may also have a loose oversight structure. The CCX currently has a functioning offset commodity standard, but suffers from lack of transparency and public accountability.

Allowing multiple standards of varying quality could . . . sow confusion and skepticism among the buying public, a process that already seems to be underway.

Might These Efforts Eventually Be Sufficient, Or Is There a Need for Government Oversight?

One answer to this question is "time will tell." Pieces of a full voluntary offset standard are coming together under various initiatives, and it is possible that the market will sort itself out as these pieces either fall away or become incorporated into a single program or set of programs. Currently, however, the proliferation of standards—many of which are incomplete—is creating more confusion than clarity.

This risk with a "wait and see" approach is that the market may never cohere around a single standard or program. Even fully established standards are not all alike. Differences in accounting and verification rules—especially with respect to additionality—can significantly affect the "quality" of carbon offsets offered to the market. Many would argue that it is not necessary to have unified quality standards, and that buyers should be able to discriminate between different quality offsets according to their needs. But given the complexity of carbon offsets as a commodity, it is not clear that typical consumers could effectively distinguish "good" quality from "bad"—especially unsophisticated buyers in the retail offset market. Allowing multiple standards of varying quality could just as easily sow confusion and skepticism among the buying public, a process that already seems to be underway.

[Carbon offsets are] a commodity . . . to benefit the public good by helping to mitigate climate change. This alone argues for public oversight.

The consequences of skepticism about the voluntary offset market are hard to predict. In the extreme case, the risk is that it could cause the voluntary market to dissolve and foster opposition to the development of mandatory offset programs. This could mean the loss of significant low-cost opportunities for mitigating climate change. Avoiding this outcome may require some kind of government oversight to ensure a minimum level of consumer protection in the voluntary carbon offset.

Ultimately, the government's focus should be on developing strong mandatory offset programs that incorporate all three required elements of a standard. As mentioned above, the true value of the voluntary market may be as a proving ground for innovative project types not incorporated in a mandatory regime. At the end of the day, however, we are still talking about a commodity whose primary purpose is to benefit the public good by helping to mitigate climate change. This alone argues for public oversight in shaping the standards that define the commodity's quality.

States Are Calling for the Federal Trade Commission to Study and Regulate Voluntary U.S. Carbon Trading

Elliot Burg and David A. Zonana

Elliot Burg is an assistant attorney general for the Vermont Attorney General's Office, and David A. Zonana is a deputy attorney general for the California Attorney General's Office.

On behalf of the Offices of Attorney General of the States of Arkansas, California, Connecticut, Delaware, Illinois, Maine, Mississippi, New Hampshire, Oklahoma, and Vermont ("the States"), we are writing to comment, from a consumer protection standpoint, on the issue of carbon offsets and renewable energy certificates.

Introduction

According to the Nobel Peace Prize-winning scientists of the Intergovernmental Panel on Climate Change (the IPCC) [a scientific body created by the United Nations to evaluate climate change], "there is *very high confidence* that the net effect of human activities since 1750 has been one of warming" and that "discernible human influences extend beyond average temperature to other aspects of climate." In this century, melting ice caps, rising sea levels, increased desertification, and consequent human dislocation and civil strife are expected to intensify absent strong and concerted action to lower greenhouse gas emissions from human activity. In the words of Ban Ki-Moon, Secretary General of the United Nations, "slowing—and reversing—these threats [of climate change] are the defining challenge of our age." And, the experts tell us, we have very little time to take decisive action.

Elliot Burg and David A. Zonana, Letter to Federal Trade Commission Re: Carbon Offset Workshop—Comment, Project No. P074207, January 25, 2008. http://ag.ca.gov.

In the United States, public concern over climate change is driving people and businesses to look for ways to address the problem, including reducing individual and corporate "carbon footprints"—thus reaping the reward of personal satisfaction or enhanced sales. In partial response to this growing concern, new global markets in carbon offsets and renewable energy certificates (RECs) have arisen. The market for the former is now estimated to exceed $100 million, but also, according to some sources, is anticipated to multiply 40-fold within the next three or four years.

As demonstrated at the recent workshop convened by the Federal Trade Commission [FTC, the nation's main consumer protection agency], these growing markets in carbon offsets and RECs raise many complex issues, some of which we address below. However, given the newness of the markets, we believe that a key first step to insuring their integrity and the protection of consumers is to undertake efforts to understand consumer perceptions of the claims made by and about these intangible products.

The market for [carbon offsets] . . . is now estimated to exceed $100 million [and] . . . is anticipated to multiply 40-fold within the next three or four years.

Ongoing Concerns

The key question of what constitutes a "real" offset of carbon emissions remains difficult to answer and the subject of much debate among stakeholders. The lack of common standards and definitions, along with the intangible nature of carbon offsets, makes it difficult if not impossible for consumers to verify that they are receiving what they paid for and creates a significant potential for deceptive claims.

Consumer marketing claims occur in two contexts: representations made in conjunction with the sale of carbon offsets (and RECs) directly to consumers; and representations made by companies about their carbon footprint or their products' or services' carbon footprint. Given reports that estimate 80 percent of offset purchases are currently made by companies, the latter subset of claims may, for the moment, be the more important.

The lack of common standards [for carbon offsets]. . . makes it difficult if not impossible for consumers to verify that they are receiving what they paid for.

Among the difficult issues embedded in the offer and sale of carbon offsets and RECs are these:

- *Additionality.* While there appears to be a conceptual consensus that carbon offsets should be "additional," there is broad disagreement over the meaning of additionality. Some stakeholders take the position that to be additional, the money raised from the sale of offsets must cause a project that would not otherwise be built to go forward ("financial additionality"). Others, including the U.S. Environmental Protection Agency, argue that it is sufficient if offsets are generated by newer projects that perform with lower emissions than the vast majority of existing projects, even if they would have gone forward without the money raised from selling offsets ("performance-based additionality"). Ultimately, the FTC must look to consumers—not stakeholders—to determine what additionality criteria will be necessary to substantiate a "carbon offset" certificate or marketing claims of "carbon neutrality" made on the basis of the purchase of carbon offsets. As the FTC noted at page 10 of its announcement in the Federal Register, the FTC's Guides "focus on the way in which consumers understand environmental claims and not necessarily the technical or scientific definition of various terms."

- *Renewable energy certificates as "carbon offsets."* There is also substantial disagreement among stakeholders on the question of whether selling a REC as a "carbon offset" is always, sometimes, or never deceptive. This debate is linked in part to the differing standards for additionality. Some regard offsets as limited to actions that directly reduce emissions from an existing practice (e.g., capturing emissions from an existing landfill), and question whether REC projects are actually displacing generation from existing fossil fuel plants as opposed to meeting an increased demand for power. For others, the question is linked to the debate over the standard for additionality, where a financial test would allow offsets to be sold only if the sale of RECs caused a renewable energy project to go forward. Here, once again, what matters most is consumer perception.

While there appears to be a conceptual consensus that carbon offsets should be "additional," there is broad disagreement over the meaning of additionality.

- *Baseline emissions.* While there is little disagreement over the need to calculate the baseline emissions from a project, for many project types there is a lack of agreed-upon standards for quantification of those baseline emissions. Rather, there are competing standards. The concern here is that this lack of common standards allows for the inflation of baselines—directly increasing the quantity of offsets—and leading to deceptive claims.

- *Benefit quantification.* Similarly, there are no common standards for quantifying the emissions reductions from offset projects. Aside from the technical differences in measurement formulas and techniques, there can be disagreements over what to count and when to count it.

- *Avoiding double-counting of offsets.* Because carbon offsets and RECs are intangible products, there must be safeguards against the double-selling of the offset or REC. Part of the solution to this problem is the creation of registries for the retirement of offsets and RECs. However, the existence of multiple registries and the possibility that the same offset or REC is being claimed by multiple entities creates uncertainty.

Because carbon offsets . . . are intangible products, there must be safeguards against the double-selling of the offset.

Recommendations

Against this background of complexity and uncertainty, the States offer the following recommendations to the Federal Trade Commission:

1. *Research on consumer perceptions.* Before any decision can be made on several key attributes of "carbon offsets" and the use of associated terms, it is necessary to understand how consumers perceive these claims and terms. What features of an offset do consumers consider to be material? What are their expectations about additionality? What do they consider to be an acceptable delay in the occurrence of sequestration or other offsetting of CO_2 emissions? How are certifications perceived? To answer these and similar questions, the FTC should seek

out pertinent consumer perception research or, in the absence of adequate information, commission such research itself.

2. *Research on the efficacy of disclosure.* There is a serious concern that given the complexity and intangibilty of offsets and RECs, ordinary consumers will not make informed decisions but rather will be heavily influenced and easily deceived by non-material information. Consider two recent studies commissioned by the FTC that cast doubt on a longstanding reliance on disclaimers as an adequate corrective to deceptive use of endorsements and testimonials. If anything, carbon offsets are much more complex and new to the public than testimonial marketing. The alternative, if warranted, would be to rely less on disclosure as a cure for deceptive practices and more on standardization of attributes and definitions.

   In seeking to determine the extent to which disclosure would be useful to consumers, one possible disclosure model to research is a uniform "Carbon Facts" box prominently placed in all marketing materials, containing basic information on the carbon offset product to which it applies, information that is comprehensible without any significant prior knowledge. Another concept to consider is requiring an initial disclosure that states, in so many words, that the best means to ensure that a consumer's contribution to global greenhouse gas emissions is reduced is to cut the individual's own emissions.

3. *Consumer education.* Pending the outcome of further study, the FTC should work to educate consumers about carbon offsets, RECs, and their relationship to climate change. Tips for consumers should at least cover the following:

a. The best means to ensure that your contribution to global greenhouse gas emissions is reduced is to cut your own emissions. (Include advice on where consumers can go to calculate their carbon footprint and get tips on how to cut their emissions.)

b. As state or federal governments create greenhouse gas caps, consumers may want to investigate purchasing from these recognized programs.

c. When purchasing a carbon offset or REC, look for disclosures that discuss the following:

    i. The name, location and ownership of the project(s) to which your money is going;

    ii. Why this project was chosen by the seller;

    iii. Why this project is not "business as usual" or already required by law;

    iv. How the emissions reductions are measured and monitored;

    v. Whether the reductions are verified by an independent source;

    vi. Whether there are safeguards to prevent the emissions reduction from being sold twice;

    vii. When the emissions reductions will occur and what happens if they do not occur; and

    viii. Whether there are additional environmental benefits from the project.

d. There is broad disagreement over whether, in order for a carbon offset to be real and additional, (i) its sale must cause a project that would not otherwise be built to go forward, or (ii) it is enough that a project that generates offsets is among the lowest emitting in its class—even if the project would have gone forward without the sales of offsets.

e. When electricity is generated from a source that does not emit greenhouse gases (e.g., wind, solar, small hydro), the generator may sell the electricity and its emissions attributes jointly as zero emissions power, or as two separate products: (i) generic electricity (with no representation of its environmental characteristics); and (ii) a renewable energy credit or REC. There is disagreement over whether a renewable energy credit or REC should be considered a "carbon offset."

Pending the outcome of further study, the FTC should work to educate consumers about carbon offsets . . . and their relationship to climate change.

---

4. *Interim enforcement.* Also pending the outcome of further study, the FTC should act to enforce its existing Guides for the Use of Environmental Marketing Claims ("the Guides") to address overly general or broad representations relating to carbon offsets and RECs. . . .

Likewise, the FTC should presently enforce the requirement of substantiation in connection with such claims as those relating to project description, baseline and emission reduction calculations, ownership (no double selling), independent verification, and ongoing monitoring. Substantiation of a "carbon offset" should require competent and reliable evidence of a number of other characteristics, including:

a. Evidence tracing the claimed emission reduction or carbon sequestration back to a specific project or projects;

b. Evidence that the project, or the practices employed at the project to reduce emissions, have not been undertaken for the purpose of complying with any existing laws or regulations;

c. Evidence that the resulting emissions reduction or carbon sequestration is not being claimed or sold more than once;

d. Evidence that the projects or practices are actually carried out and are permanent, which might include evidence of monitoring and verification;

e. Evidence that the project or the practices do not result in "leakage," or, in other words, an increase in emissions elsewhere; and

f. Reliable scientific evidence—as defined in the FTC's Green Guides—of the measurement of the emissions reduction or sequestration claimed, which would include evidence of both baseline calculations and emission or sequestration data.

We need to ensure, by law, that carbon offsets are real, additional, verifiable, [and] enforceable.

A December 2006 report from [the nonprofit group] Clean Air Cool Planet entitled *A Consumer's Guide to Retail Carbon Offset Providers* summed up the market in carbon offsets this way: "In the absence of a clear quality standard for offsets, a reliable provider certification process, or effective disclosure and verification protocols, the retail market remains a 'consumer beware' market." However, the FTC, and by extension, the States, can and need to do better than to preside over a "consumer beware" market. Particularly given the rising importance of—perhaps the *need for*—carbon offset-type products in the market, we cannot afford to settle for less. Instead, we need to ensure, by law, that carbon offsets are real, additional, verifiable, enforceable, and accompanied by some system that will permit average consumers to make informed decisions as to whether and what to buy.

The U.S. Congress Should Pass a Carbon Offset Certification Process

Center for American Progress

The Center for American Progress is a public policy think tank located in Washington, D.C.

Legislation under debate [in 2008] . . . and proposed by Sen. Joseph Lieberman (I-CT) and John Warner (R-VA) would establish a national carbon cap-and-trade program that would regulate carbon emissions and auction emission permits to industries. Industries, in turn, could use those permits to pay for the right to pollute or trade them with other polluting industries if they are able to reduce their greenhouse gas emissions below the allowed limit.

An often overlooked but nonetheless controversial component of this proposed cap-and-trade system is a provision that will help emitters to meet their emission reduction targets, in part, by purchasing additional carbon "offset" credits. Polluting industries can either reduce their emissions by making changes in their operations (employing clean technologies or upgrading efficiency) or by investing in offsets. These offset credits would be purchased from projects and programs that reduce emissions in emitting sectors that are currently not regulated by the cap-and-trade system. For example, some of these carbon-reducing enterprises include investments in renewable energy, energy efficiency, or agricultural and forestry land management practices that reduce emissions.

"Carbon Offsets 101: What Are Carbon Offsets, and What Would a Successful Carbon Offsets Program Look Like?" Center for American Progress, March 3, 2008. This material was created by the Center for American Progress. www.americanprogress.org. Reproduced by permission.

What Are Carbon Offsets?

Carbon offsetting is the act of mitigating greenhouse gas emissions by purchasing credits from projects and programs that reduce emissions from sectors currently unregulated by the cap on emissions. In the current offset market, consumers, for example, may purchase carbon offsets to compensate for greenhouse gas emissions caused by personal air travel or driving, thereby "neutralizing" their carbon emissions.

Carbon offsets are typically measured in tons of CO_2-equivalents, or CO_2e, and are bought and sold through a number of international brokers, online retailers, and trading platforms. Most companies charge \$5 to \$20 per ton of CO_2e offset.

Because there is currently no system to regulate offsets, the voluntary market is awash in competing protocols and standards, and confusion reigns.

The Problem with Offsets

A barrage of critical news reports has raised serious questions about the integrity of the carbon offsets that are sold in the unregulated U.S. market. It turns out that some offset dollars are being collected for projects that already have been financed independently, arguably doing no additional environmental good. And even when offset dollars appear to be invested wisely, consumers have no way to check whether projects are actually producing the promised reductions in greenhouse gas emissions.

Because there is currently no system to regulate offsets, the voluntary market is awash in competing protocols and standards, and confusion reigns. Some providers are committing to follow specific protocols or standards, such as the Kyoto Protocol's Clean Development Mechanism, which has received criticism for granting legitimacy to dubious technologies. No

U.S. government standards currently exist, however, and buyers have a limited ability to check whether such promises are being kept.

Congress should craft a wise carbon offset certification process as part of a mandatory cap-and-trade system.

The Solution

Congress should craft a wise carbon offset certification process as part of a mandatory cap-and-trade system. A well-designed carbon offset program must ensure that entities selling offsets can meet rigorous, uniform standards and verify their emission reductions. The Environmental Protection Agency should therefore step in and outline consistent methodologies and protocols for offset certification in order to ensure the program's success.

In a recent CAP [Center for American Progress, a progressive think tank] publication, "Getting Credit for Going Green" we outline recommendations for a robust offsets program to ensure real and verifiable emission reductions. A main component of this program includes establishing two categories of offsets, Tier 1 and Tier 2:

- *Tier 1 offsets*—otherwise known as Compliance Credits—will be certified by the EPA and will meet stringent measurement, verification, and permanence requirements via the application of rigorous EPA methodologies and protocols.

  Polluting industries will only be able to meet 15 percent of their emission requirements with Tier 1 compliance credits. These credits would count as reductions contributing to meeting the overall cap on U.S. emissions.

Individuals will also be able to purchase these Tier 1 compliance credits in the voluntary market. Because individuals are not regulated entities under the cap, these Tier 1 compliance credits would count as additional emission reductions beyond those required by the cap.

- *Tier 2 offsets* will comprise the Targeted Carbon Reduction Program. This Tier 2 program would include program- or project-based activities that may not satisfy the stringent tests required to earn Tier 1 compliance credits but still reduce emissions. These activities would earn other financial rewards, including tax credits, rebates, grants, or other financial incentives.

   Emission reductions resulting from the Tier 2 program would count as additional emission reductions beyond those required by the cap.

   Once Tier 2 programs develop a track record and more data has been collected on their resulting emission reductions, some of them may qualify to move up into Tier 1, where they can generate marketable compliance credits. In this way, Tier 2 may serve as an "incubator" of projects and programs that ultimately may qualify for compliance credit status under Tier 1.

One of the benefits of such an offset program is that it can encourage emissions reductions in sectors that are not currently covered under a cap-and-trade program. This type of comprehensive offset program would provide more information about the nature and scope of unregulated emissions and set the stage for their potential official inclusion in a cap-and-trade program at a future date.

A strictly regulated offset program would provide entities and individuals who are interested in reducing their carbon footprints with a new, highly credible means to do so. It will encourage both offset buyers and sellers to become more efficient by ensuring that credits provide a real carbon offset and are retired from the market once they are purchased, thereby making them unavailable for use by other regulated entities under the cap. This prospect provides a strong rationale for moving forward with a stringent two-tiered offset program as part of a mandatory cap-and-trade scheme.

The Gold Standard Can Provide Quality Assurance for the Voluntary Carbon Offset Market

WWF

WWF is a multinational nature conservation organization active in 100 countries around the world.

The Gold Standard was created to ensure top quality projects under a Kyoto [referring to the Kyoto Protocol, an international treaty to cut greenhouse gas emissions] instrument, the Clean Development Mechanism (CDM) [a carbon offset program created by the Kyoto treaty]. It is the most widely endorsed quality standard for designing and implementing carbon offset projects.

The Gold Standard's main purpose is to ensure that CDM projects are both reducing carbon dioxide (CO_2) emissions and fostering sustainable development. In WWF's [World Wildlife Fund, an environmental organization] view, the Gold Standard reflects best the objectives of the CDM as defined in the Kyoto Protocol.

The Gold Standard was created to ensure top quality projects under a Kyoto [carbon offset] instrument, the Clean Development Mechanism (CDM).

An Independent Best Practice Benchmark

If designed correctly, CDM and Joint Implementation (JI) projects [another type of carbon offset program under Kyoto] can play a valuable role in promoting the spread of sustainable energy technologies both within and outside the industrialized world.

The key phrase is *if designed correctly*.

The Gold Standard: Quality Standards for the CDM and JI, is designed to be an independent best practice benchmark for CDM and JI greenhouse gas offset projects.

The CDM Gold Standard is a new innovative NGO [nongovernmental organization] product which has been designed to promote a sizeable market in 'quality' certified emissions reductions and emissions reductions units from CDM projects. The Standard itself is a project methodology, fully consistent with the CDM Executive Board's Project Design Document, which provides assurance that CDM projects will deliver what they are supposed to deliver—real emissions reductions and a clear contribution towards sustainable development.

It offers project developers a tool with which they can ensure that the CDM and JI deliver credible projects with real environmental benefits and, in so doing, give confidence to host countries and the public that projects represent new and additional investments in sustainable energy services.

At Carbon Expo 2006, the Gold Standard launched its methodology for voluntary offset projects, a simplified version of the CDM Gold Standard.

Gold Standard Architecture

The Gold Standard is built on the basic architecture of CDM projects and is in line with the rules of the CDM Executive Board, the official body within the UN [United Nations] approving CDM projects. This allows project developers to use the same tool (the CDM approval form) but in its expanded form for CDM Gold Standard projects.

Using the Gold Standard methodology marginally increases development costs compared to a standard CDM project. But there are advantages: better project preparation means that proper stakeholder consultation has been conducted, the local population and environment of the project have been taken into account, and possible stumbling blocks with local initiatives have been tackled and addressed. Overall the Gold Standard methodology will lead to a better project preparation and lower project risk, which in practice also leads to financial benefits for the developer.

Voluntary Gold Standard Projects

At Carbon Expo 2006, the Gold Standard launched its methodology for voluntary offset projects, a simplified version of the CDM Gold Standard. This methodology keeps intact the basic rules of the Gold Standard but makes them more easily applicable. This methodology is, however, only available for Voluntary Emission Reductions—and it creates so-called VERs—Voluntary Emission Reduction units. To avoid problems with double accounting, this methodology, similar to the CDM, is only available for developing countries.

> *The Gold Standard for voluntary offset projects tackles the . . . need [for quality assurance] and is so far the only independent standard for quality in this market.*

What Is the Difference Between CDM and Voluntary Projects?

CDM projects are part of the Kyoto Protocol flexible mechanisms. As such they can generate credits for emission reductions that can be included in a country's official emissions accounts.

If an industrialised country has to reduce its emissions by a certain amount by a certain time (e.g. Germany X%, the Netherlands Y% by 2012) then it can at least partly cover this reduction by buying credits from CDM projects (or investing in CDM projects). CDM projects have to be in developing countries. A second system, called Joint Implementation (JI), will tackle investment in industrialised countries and . . . [came] into force [in] 2008.

CDM projects are now gaining momentum: in December 2005, there were 40 CDM-registered projects, with 500 in the pipeline. By May 2006, there were more than 176 registered projects and approximately 600 in the CDM evaluation process leading to registration.

Voluntary projects are outside the Kyoto system. Their emission reductions cannot be traded in official emission trading systems. Most offset projects to date are developed in the voluntary market and have not followed a particular standard. Small projects will find the voluntary offset market increasingly attractive because projects are mostly cheaper than under the CDM. They are attractive to companies who use offset as part of their corporate social responsibility strategy but which up to now are not legally obliged to lower their emissions. Those buyers will, however, also look for quality assurance: the Gold Standard for voluntary offset projects tackles this need and is so far the only independent standard for quality in this market.

Voluntary Carbon Trading Should Be Globally Regulated

Simon Linnett

Simon Linnett is executive vice-chairman of Rothschild, one of the world's major investment banking organizations. For the past ten years, he has been a vocal proponent of a global carbon trading system.

"An urgent global response." This was how [British economist] Nicolas Stern described the problem of carbon dioxide emissions, in his recent review of the economics of climate change. The sense of an impending crisis infuses all our debates on this issue.

The human causes of climate change are now well established. The overall measures we must take—a reduction of our emissions—is painfully obvious.

But like a group of rabbits caught in the headlights, our actual means of escape remain unclear. We know what our end goals are, but how do we get there? How can governments achieve delivery?

The [global warming] problem is literally too big for any one country to handle.

A Global Solution

The first step must be to recognise the scope of the problem. Unlike other pollutants, such as litter or nuclear waste, CO_2 emissions have impact on a global level—and only on a global level.

This means we have to deal with the issue internationally. The problem is literally too big for any one country to handle. Old alliances, divisions and 'special relationships' are a meaningless hindrance.

Only the private sector can successfully develop. . . solutions [for global warming], but only governments can provide a framework for them to be applied internationally.

I believe it is essential that governments and the private sector work together to solve the problem. As a banker, I suppose I would say that, but only such a partnership will we be able to harness what Al Gore called the multitude of little solutions, which all add up to a better outcome.

Only the private sector can successfully develop those solutions, but only governments can provide a framework for them to be applied internationally.

As a banker, I also welcome the fact that the 'cap-and-trade' system is becoming the dominant methodology for CO_2 control. Unlike taxation, or plain regulation, cap-and-trade offers the greatest scope for private sector involvement and innovation.

Furthermore, taxation and regulation can only be levied at local or national levels, whereas cap-and-trade can operate on a global level. And remember, the problem is global.

But for the private sector to participate enthusiastically in a global carbon trading market, governments must collectively establish a robust framework within which trading can occur. It must be long, loud and legal:

- Long: it is going to be around for a long time;

- Loud: it will be the dominant mechanism for sponsoring changes in behaviour and we are going to make this perfectly clear to the world's people; and

• Legal: we will enforce it through law.

Subordinating National Interests

A key implication of creating a legal yet global system of trading, is the loss of sovereignty it implies. Governments must be prepared to allow some subordination of national interests to this world initiative, on the issue of emissions. This need not mean a new system of government, above individual nations.

But it would mean a change to the way treaties are agreed and worded. Instead of saying "we will cut emissions by x per cent by date y" (pledges which are inevitably broken), such statements will have to morph to "we will make our contribution to a scheme which cuts, across certain industries and gases, emissions by x per cent by date y."

The European nations already do this, on certain issues, yielding sovereignty to the EU. And in time, the EU itself will eventually have to yield to a larger body—one which includes the economic powerhouses of India and China.

The cynicism that greets such programmes is well known, since the Asian economies seem bent on rapid expansion. However, I believe that both India and China will soon recognise the benefits of joining a global carbon trading scheme.

First, a properly constituted, one-member-one-vote system would mean that they have a proper 'say'. More importantly, since the allocation of the emissions cap might trend towards recognising world populations rather than current levels of emission, both countries would stand to gain a great deal.

Emissions trading could establish a new world order for a sustainable planet, one based on the sharing of the earth's ability to absorb harmful emissions.

If emissions trading could expand into different areas of economic activity, so too could its message. When an individual receives an electricity bill, they will come to know what the cost of turning on the gas or a light was to the environment.

Perhaps they will gain a new appreciation of their burden on the broader world. Similarly, if the scheme were to expand geographically to include India, China and, ultimately, the US, so too could the prospect be realised of such allowances becoming the reserve currency of the world, taking over that role held for most of the 20th century by gold.

So emissions trading could establish a new world order for a sustainable planet, one based on the sharing of the earth's ability to absorb harmful emissions. To allocate that 'resource' fully and properly will, in turn, require resourcefulness and imagination across the globe.

Organizations to Contact

Carbon Neutral Digest
E-mail: matt@carbonneutraldigest.com
Web site: www.carbonneutraldigest.com

Carbon Neutral Digest is a Web site that offers information about becoming carbon neutral. The site provides an up to date list of all U.S.-based organizations that offer voluntary carbon offsets, a description of their practices, and an explanation of what is involved with each offset project. The Web site also offers access to interviews conducted with major leaders in the carbon neutral industry.

Carbon Trade Watch
Transnational Institute, Amsterdam   1001 LD
   The Netherlands
+ 31 20 662 66 08 • Fax: + 31 20 675 71 76
Web site: www.carbontradewatch.org

Carbon Trade Watch is an international organization that seeks to research and monitor the impact of global carbon trading on society and the environment. Its Web site is a source for numerous articles and information critical or skeptical about the value of carbon trading and carbon offsets. The site also provides links to other organizations throughout the world that focus on climate justice issues.

Carbonfund.org
1320 Fenwick Lane, Suite 206, Silver Spring, MD   20910
(240) 247-0630
E-mail: info@carbonfund.org
Web site: www.carbonfund.org

Carbonfund.org is a nonprofit provider of carbon offsets for individuals, businesses, and organizations. The group offers three types of carbon offset projects: renewable energy, energy efficiency, and reforestation. It also provides education about climate change and advocates for reducing carbon emissions. The group's Web site is a source of information about climate change and carbon offsets, and it includes a carbon calculator to help people estimate their carbon footprints.

Clean Air—Cool Planet

100 Market Street, S. 104, Plymouth, NH   03801
(603)422-6464 • Fax: (603)422-6441
Web site: www.cleanair-coolplanet.org

Clean Air-Cool Planet (CA-CP) is a New England-based organization dedicated to finding and promoting solutions to global warming. The group helps companies, campuses, communities, and science centers throughout the Northeast United States reduce their carbon emissions. The group's Web site is an invaluable source of information about climate change, carbon offset programs, and related information. Publications include *Getting to Zero: Defining Corporate Carbon Neutrality* and *A Consumer's Guide to Retail Carbon Offset Providers*, and the Web site also includes news articles and links to other Web sites and publications.

Climate Action Network

1326 14th Street NW, Washington, DC   20005
(202)609-9846 • Fax: (202)536-5503
Web site: www.climatenetwork.org

The Climate Action Network (CAN) is a worldwide network of more than 430 nongovernmental organizations (NGOs) working to promote government and individual action to limit human-induced climate change to ecologically sustainable levels. This Web site offers a non-profit perspective on the latest news from international climate negotiations. Among the publications are explanations of the Kyoto Protocol and its carbon trading mechanisms, and the site also contains links to a number of other Web sites on climate change.

Climate Solutions
219 Legion Way SW, Suite 201, Olympia, WA 98501
(360)352-1763
Web site: http://climatesolutions.org

Climate Solutions is a nonprofit organization that seeks to find and accelerate practical and profitable solutions to global warming in the U.S. Northwest. The Web site provides useful information about many aspects of the global warming problem and possible solutions, including articles and publications on carbon offsets.

Climate Trust
65 SW Yamhill Street, Suite 400, Portland, OR 97204
(503)238-1915
Web site: www.climatetrust.org

The Climate Trust is a nonprofit organization based in Oregon that offers various carbon offset projects for sale to individuals, businesses, and power companies. Projects include small-scale wind, tree planting, and projects geared toward increasing energy efficiency. The group has a long history of advocating for carbon offset and other climate change initiatives. Its Web site provides public access to numerous press releases, news items, and reports, as well as back issues of its twice-yearly newsletter, *Climate Trust Times*.

Intergovernmental Panel on Climate Change (IPCC)
+41-22-730-8208/84
E-mail: IPCC-Sec@wmo.int

The IPCC is a scientific intergovernmental body set up by the United Nations Environment Programme (UNEP) to provide policy makers and others interested in climate change with an objective source of information about climate change. The IPCC does not conduct any research or monitor climate related data; its role is only to assess on a comprehensive, objective, open, and transparent basis the latest scientific, technical, and socio-economic literature produced worldwide relevant to the understanding of the risk of human-induced climate change, its observed and projected impacts, and options for adaptation and mitigation. On this site, researchers can find IPCC reports detailing the latest scientific information about the extent of climate change.

My Climate

Sustainable Travel International, Boulder, CO   80306

(800)276-7764

E-mail: info@sustainabletravel.com

Web site: www. sustainabletravelinternational.org

My Climate is a nonprofit organization and is the exclusive provider of "myclimate™" carbon offsets in the United States, a service that helps people and companies fight global climate change by investing in certified or verified carbon offset projects that help to neutralize the negative impacts of their air and ground travel, home energy consumption, and hotel stays. The group publishes a newsletter, the *Responsible Travel Report*. The Web site offers various publications, including press releases, fact sheets, and news articles about global warming and carbon trading.

Native Energy

30 Kimball Avenue, Suite 301, South Burlington, VT   05403

(800)924-6826

E-mail: info@nativeenergy.com

Web site: www.nativeenergy.com

Native Energy is a carbon offset company that helps individuals and businesses invest in Native American, farmer-owned, and community based renewable energy projects that create social, economic, and environmental benefits. The group's Web site contains information about global warming and carbon offsets and provides access to a list of news articles about the company and to the company's monthly newsletter.

RealClimate
E-mail: contrib@realclimate.org
Web site: www.realclimate.org

RealClimate is a commentary Web site on climate science run by working climate scientists for the benefit of the interested public and journalists. It seeks to provide a quick response to developing stories and provide the context sometimes missing in mainstream commentary. Discussion is restricted to scientific topics and does not address any political or economic implications of the science. This Web site provides extensive information about global warming; it describes itself as a one-stop link for resources that people can use to get up to speed on the issue of climate change.

U.S. Environmental Protection Agency (EPA)
Climate Change Division, Washington, DC   20460
(202) 343-9990
E-mail: climatechange@epa.gov
Web site: www.epa.gov

The EPA is the main federal agency in the United States responsible for environmental policy. The EPA's Climate Change Web site offers comprehensive information on the issue of climate change, including publications on carbon offsets and analyses of recently proposed legislative carbon trading programs. The site also offers a database of climate change related sites.

Bibliography

Books

Ricardo Bayon, Amanda Hawn, Katherine Hamilton, and Al Gore — *Voluntary Carbon Markets: An International Business Guide to What They Are and How They Work.* London: Earthscan Publications Ltd., 2007.

Mark Brassington — *How to Go Carbon Neutral: A Practical Guide to Treading More Lightly upon the Earth.* Oxford, UK: How to Books Ltd., 2008.

Andres R. Edwards and David W. Orr — *The Sustainability Revolution: Portrait of a Paradigm Shift.* Gabriola Island, BC, Canada: New Society Publishers, 2005.

Daniel C. Esty and Andrew S. Winston — *Green to Gold: How Smart Companies Use Environmental Strategy to Innovate, Create Value, and Build Competitive Advantage.* New Haven, CT: Yale University Press, 2006.

David Gershon — *Low Carbon Diet: A 30 Day Program to Lose 5,000 Pounds—Be Part of the Global Warming Solution!* Woodstock, NY: Empowerment Institute, 2006.

Chris Goodall — *How to Live a Low-Carbon Life: The Individuals Guide to Stopping Climate Change.* London: Earthscan Publications Ltd., 2007.

Nancy S. Grant   *The Pocket Idiot's Guide to Your Carbon Footprint*. Royersford, PA: Alpha, 2008.

Jonathan Harrington   *The Climate Diet: How You Can Cut Carbon, Cut Costs and Save the Planet*. London: Earthscan Publications Ltd., 2008.

Andrew J. Hoffman   *Carbon Strategies: How Leading Companies Are Reducing Their Climate Change Footprint*. Ann Arbor, MI: University of Michigan Press, 2007.

Sonia Labatt and Rodney R. White   *Carbon Finance: The Financial Implications of Climate Change*. Hoboken, NJ: Wiley, 2007.

Larry Lohmann, ed.   *Carbon Trading: A Critical Conversation on Climate Change, Privatisation and Power*. Uppsala, Sweden: Dag Hammarskjold Foundation, Durban Group for Climate Justice, and The Corner House, 2006.

William McDonough and Michael Braungart   *Cradle to Cradle: Remaking the Way We Make Things*. New York: North Point Press, 2002.

Ian Swingland   *Capturing Carbon and Conserving Biodiversity: The Market Approach*. London: Earthscan Publications Ltd., 2003.

T.H. Tietenberg   *Emissions Trading: Principles and Practice.* Washington, D.C.: RFF Press, 2006.

Farhana Yamin   *Climate Change and Carbon Markets: A Handbook of Emissions Reduction Mechanisms.* London: Earthscan Publications Ltd., 2005.

Joanna Yarrow   *How to Reduce Your Carbon Footprint: 365 Simple Ways to Save Energy, Resources, and Money.* San Francisco, CA: Chronicle Books, 2008.

Periodicals

Adam Bumpus   "Carbon Offsets," *Geography Review,* Vol. 21, No. 4, April 2008, p. 24.

Business Week   "Another Inconvenient Truth: Behind the Feel-Good Hype of Carbon Offsets, Some of the Deals Don't Deliver," March 26, 2007. www.businessweek.com/magazine/content/07_13/b4027057.htm.

Melissa Checker   "Carbon Offsets: More Harm Than Good?" *Counterpunch,* August 27, 2008. www.counterpunch.org/checker08272008.html.

The Economist   "Carbon Offsets," August 3, 2006. www.economist.com/opinion/displaystory.cfm?story_id=7252897.

Ecos "Buyers' Guide to Carbon Offset Providers," Vol. 142, April–May 2008, p. 7.

Jesse Ellison "Save the Planet, Lose the Guilt," *Newsweek*, July 7–15, 2008. www.newsweek.com/id/143701.

David A. Fahrenthold "Value of U.S. House's Carbon Offsets Is Murky: Some Question Effectiveness of $89,000 Purchase to Balance Out Greenhouse Gas Emissions," *The Washington Post*, January 28, 2008, p. A01. www.washingtonpost.com/wp-dyn/content/story/2008/01/28/ST2008012800764.html.

Pallavi Gogoi "Carbon Offsets Take Flight," *Business Week*, March 24, 2008. www.businessweek.com/bwdaily/dnflash/content/mar2008/db20080321_437700.htm.

Isabelle Groc "Giving Back to the Friendly Skies: Carbon Offsets Can Be a Good Way to Reduce Your Traveling Carbon Footprint, But Be Wary of Green Scams," *PC Magazine*, Vol. 27, No. 5, April 2008, p. 20.

Marc Gunther "In Defense of Carbon Offsets," *The Huffinton Post*, August 7, 2007. www.huffingtonpost.com/marc-gunther/in-defense-of-carbon-offs_b_59423.html.

Unmesh Kher   "Pay for Your Carbon Sins," *TIME*, March 27, 2007. http://www.time.com/ time/specials/2007/environment/ article/0,28804,1602354_16 03074_1603737,00.html.

Martin LaMonica   "Carbon Offset Providers Jockey for Credibility," *CNET*, February 26, 2008. http://news.cnet.com/ 8301-11128_3-9879576-54.html.

Jason Mark   "Flying into Trouble: Where Are Carbon Offsets Taking Us?" *Earth Island Journal*, Vol. 23, No. 2, Summer 2008, p. 44.

Katharine Mieszkowski "Paying Off Our Global Warming Sins: Buying Credits to Offset Our Driving and Flying Is Helping to Reduce Greenhouse Gases. But Is the "Carbon-Neutral" Movement Really Enough?" *Salon*, May 26, 2008. www.salon.com/news/feature/ 2006/05/26/offsets/.

New Internationalist "Carbon Offsets—The Facts," No. 391, July 2006, www.newint.org/ features/2006/07/01/carbon-offsets-facts/.

Louise Story   "F.T.C. Asks if Carbon-Offset Money Is Well Spent," *New York Times*, January 9, 2008. www.nytimes.com/ 2008/01/09/business/09offsets.html? _r=1&oref=slogin.

A.C. Thompson   "Don't Bet on Offsets," *The Nation*,
and Duane Moles   April 19, 2007. www.thenation.com/
                    doc/20070507/thompson_moles.

Paul Tolme   "Consumers and Carbon," *Newsweek*,
                    Vol. 152, No. 4, July 28, 2008, p. 55.

Bryan Walsh   "How to Save the Planet and Make
                    Money Doing It," *TIME*, April 20,
                    2008. www.time.com/time/health/
                    article/0,8599,1732518,00.html.

Mark Wexler   "Navigating Through Carbon
                    Confusion," *National Wildlife*,
                    Vol. 46, No. 1, December–January
                    2008, p. 12.

Daphne Wysham   "Why Carbon Offsets Backfire,"
                    Mother Jones, July/August 2008.
                    www.motherjones.com/news/
                    outfront/2008/07/
                    outfront-location-location.html.

Index